COMPUTER SCIENCE, TECHNOLOGY AND APPLICATIONS

PERFORMANCE MODELLING TECHNIQUES FOR PARALLEL SUPERCOMPUTING APPLICATIONS

COMPUTER SCIENCE, TECHNOLOGY AND APPLICATIONS

Additional books in this series can be found on Nova's website under the Series tab.

Additional E-books in this series can be found on Nova's website under the E-book tab.

COMPUTER SCIENCE, TECHNOLOGY AND APPLICATIONS

PERFORMANCE MODELLING TECHNIQUES FOR PARALLEL SUPERCOMPUTING APPLICATIONS

D. A. GROVE
AND
P. D. CODDINGTON
EDITORS

Novinka
Nova Science Publishers, Inc.
New York

Copyright © 2010 by Nova Science Publishers, Inc.

All rights reserved. No part of this book may be reproduced, stored in a retrieval system or transmitted in any form or by any means: electronic, electrostatic, magnetic, tape, mechanical photocopying, recording or otherwise without the written permission of the Publisher.

For permission to use material from this book please contact us:
Telephone 631-231-7269; Fax 631-231-8175
Web Site: http://www.novapublishers.com

NOTICE TO THE READER

The Publisher has taken reasonable care in the preparation of this book, but makes no expressed or implied warranty of any kind and assumes no responsibility for any errors or omissions. No liability is assumed for incidental or consequential damages in connection with or arising out of information contained in this book. The Publisher shall not be liable for any special, consequential, or exemplary damages resulting, in whole or in part, from the readers' use of, or reliance upon, this material. Any parts of this book based on government reports are so indicated and copyright is claimed for those parts to the extent applicable to compilations of such works.

Independent verification should be sought for any data, advice or recommendations contained in this book. In addition, no responsibility is assumed by the publisher for any injury and/or damage to persons or property arising from any methods, products, instructions, ideas or otherwise contained in this publication.

This publication is designed to provide accurate and authoritative information with regard to the subject matter covered herein. It is sold with the clear understanding that the Publisher is not engaged in rendering legal or any other professional services. If legal or any other expert assistance is required, the services of a competent person should be sought. FROM A DECLARATION OF PARTICIPANTS JOINTLY ADOPTED BY A COMMITTEE OF THE AMERICAN BAR ASSOCIATION AND A COMMITTEE OF PUBLISHERS.

LIBRARY OF CONGRESS CATALOGING-IN-PUBLICATION DATA

Grove, D. A. (Duncan A.)
Performance modelling techniques for parallel supercomputing applications / D.A. Grove and P.D. Coddington.
 p. cm.
Includes index.
ISBN 978-1-60692-269-9 (softcover)
1. Parallel processing (Electronic computers)--Mathematical models. 2. Parallel programming (Computer science)--Mathematical models. 3. Supercomputers--Mathematical models. I. Coddington, P. D. (Paul D.) II. Title.
 QA76.58.G76 2009
 004'.35--dc22
                    2009008033

Published by Nova Science Publishers, Inc. ✦ New York

Contents

Preface   vii

1 Introduction   1

2 Amdahl   5

3 Fortune and Wylie   7

4 Hoare; Milner; Alur and Dill   9

5 Valiant   13

6 Hockney   15

7 Saavedra and Smith   17

8 Culler *et al.*   19

9 Grama *et al.*   21

10 Adve   23

11 Singh *et al.*   27

12 Mehra *et al.*   29

13 Parashar and Hariri   33

14 Skillicorn	37
15 Crovella and LeBlanc	41
16 Mraz; Tabe *et al.*	43
17 Clement, Quinn and Steed	47
18 Islam	49
19 Jonkers	51
20 van Gemund	55
21 Labarta and Girona *et al.*	61
22 Dunlop and Hey *et al.*	63
23 Becker *et al.*	67
24 Gautama	69
25 Tam and Wang	71
26 Kranzlmüller and Schaubschläger	73
27 Magnusson *et al.*; Hughes *et al.*	77
28 Grove and Coddington	79
29 SciDAC PERC and PERI	85
30 Conclusion	87
References	89
Index	117

Preface

Ever since the invention of the computer, users have demanded more and more computational power to tackle increasingly complex problems. A common means of increasing the amount of computational power available for solving a problem is to use parallel computing. Unfortunately, however, creating efficient parallel programs is notoriously difficult.

In addition to all of the well-known problems that are associated with constructing a good serial algorithm, there are a number of problems specifically associated with constructing a good parallel algorithm. These mainly revolve around ensuring that all processors are kept busy and that they have timely access to the data that they require. Unfortunately, however, controlling a number of processors operating in parallel can be exponentially more complicated than controlling one processor. Furthermore, unlike data placement in serial programs, where sophisticated compilation techniques that optimise cache behaviour and memory interleaving are common, optimising data placement throughout the vastly more complex memory hierarchy present in parallel computers is often left to the parallel application programmer. All of these problems are compounded by the large number of parallel computing architectures that exist, because they often exhibit vastly different performance characteristics, which makes writing well-optimised, portable code especially difficult.

The primary weapon against these problems in a parallel programmer's or parallel computer architect's arsenal is – or at least should be – the art of performance prediction. This chapter provides a historical exposition of over four decades of research into techniques for modelling the performance of computer programs running on parallel computers.

The majority of the text in this book was written while the first author was a PhD student in the Department of Computer Science at the University of Adelaide. He greatly acknowleges the support he received from the University as well as the Australian Government's Advanced Computational Systems and Research Data Networks CRCs during this time. The remaining material, found in Chapter 29, was added after the first author joined the Australian Government's Defence Science & Technology Organisation. He would like to acknowledge DSTO's continued support of his research.

Chapter 1

Introduction

Throughout the genesis of parallel computing in the 1960s and 1970s, research developments in parallel algorithms were strongly grounded in theory. The main early formalisms for parallel processing were summarised in a book by Peterson [183]. In particular, he identified the work of Dijkstra on P/V constructs in 1965 [66], Karp and Miller on computation graphs in 1966 [137], Bredt on finite state machines in 1970 [35], and extended petri net models in 1974 by Peterson and Bredt [182], Agerwala [3] and Lipton *et al.* [148]. Although these works have provided robust formalisms that continue to serve as a useful basis for modelling parallel processing, the computational requirements of solving these models grow exponentially with the size of a system. This makes them practically applicable to only relatively small systems or where very high costs in terms of solution time or resource requirements are acceptable (see Sections 4 and 27).

In the 1980s significant research attention was focused on practical ways of devising efficient parallel algorithms using the Parallel Random Access Machine (PRAM) model and closely related variants (see Section 3). These models require an algorithm to be completely described in terms of instructions that control individual memory accesses. This allowed researchers to understand the very fine-grained characteristics of the parallel algorithms that they were studying. Unfortunately, the underlying machine models upon which these studies were based were unable to accurately reflect the complexity of the physical processes that occur in a parallel computer system. Although many extensions to the PRAM model were suggested to try and overcome its various limitations, these were largely unsuccessful because the numerous modifications could not be effectively unified.

During the late 1980s and early 1990s researchers began contemplating new ways to tackle the problem of modelling the performance of parallel programs. New methodologies were devised that allowed a direct evaluation of performance from the structure of source code (such as those discussed in Sections 5, 8 and 15). In many cases the programming structures that these techniques encouraged allowed performance to be modelled using several parameters and simple equations. Although these methodologies allowed the creation of efficient programs with predictable performance, the techniques were not amenable to the increasing number of irregular problems that high performance computing was aiming to solve and which required more complicated control structures.

To deal with these more complicated programs, researchers turned to statistical and Markov modelling techniques to try to estimate the performance characteristics of a program. While these approaches were relatively successful in modelling specific situations, they suffered from two problems. The first of these was the high computational requirement of these approaches because solution techniques were generally of exponential order, although solution requirements were potentially less than those generated by the very early techniques mentioned previously. Still, these techniques remain in use today for certain well defined problems. The second difficulty was more significant: these techniques did not really help a programmer to understand their parallel program better or provide insight into ways that would allow them to improve it.

More recently, modelling research has favoured techniques that involve a detailed understanding of the performance of small chunks of code (see Sections 7, 12, 13 and 14) rather than a general notion of the average performance of macroscopic blocks of code. In a way, this is very similar to the early PRAM modelling techniques, although significant advances have been made in understanding the general causes of performance degradation in parallel programs (see Sections 10, 11, 15, 16, 17, 18, 19, 20, 24 and 25). This philosophy has encouraged the development of performance modelling tools able to tackle arbitrary parallel programs (see Sections 21, 22 and 26).

Research in the field of performance modelling for parallel programs has still to settle on an appropriate level of abstraction. At one extreme, a complete model of every intricacy of a problem is intractable and, what is more, it will not usually increase a programmer's insight into a problem. At the other extreme, reducing the performance of a program to a number of simple equations (such as the techniques discussed in Sections 2, 6, 9, 12 and 23) is too simplistic and likewise does not significantly help a programmer see ways to improve a solution to a problem. It seems that the most promising modelling techniques lie somewhere in between. Recent work taking such an approach is described in 28.

A convenient way of providing an overview of the performance modelling of parallel programs is to present a historical summary of research that has been carried out. This is possible because most of the advances that have been made occurred sequentially, or addressed independent issues. The following sections chronicle the major contributions that have been made, so far, to the field of performance modelling of parallel programs.

Chapter 2

Amdahl

The earliest model commonly used to determine the performance bounds of parallel programs was devised by Amdahl in 1967 [8]. When applied to parallel processing, this model can be used to compute the maximum possible speedup S of the parallel version of a program compared with a corresponding serial version of the same program using the formula:

$$S(P) \leq \left(f + \frac{1-f}{P}\right)^{-1}$$

where f is the serial fraction of the program and P is the number of processors available to the parallel version. The serial fraction of a code represents the run-time that is associated with any parts of the code that cannot be parallelised and must therefore be run on only one processor.

Chapter 3

Fortune and Wylie

In 1978, Fortune and Wylie [88] described an abstract model of parallel computation based on the Parallel Random Access Machine (PRAM). Early models related to the PRAM were described by Schwartz [214] and Goldschlager [100]. The PRAM aimed to provide a general model of parallel computation, in contrast to a special purpose model of parallel computation that could fully exploit the available hardware. Unfortunately, special purpose models were rarely portable to other situations. The general model provided by the PRAM aimed to abstract over the details of specific machines and programming styles and instead focus on the inherent parallelism available in a given problem, but possibly at the cost of optimisations based on full knowledge of those details.

The basic PRAM is an idealised parallel processing machine, consisting of P synchronous processors communicating via shared memory. Each processor is able to execute one instruction or perform one communication operation per clock cycle. There are several families of PRAMs which are classified by the semantics used for accessing shared memory. These are: the Exclusive Read, Exclusive Write (EREW) PRAM; the Concurrent Read, Exclusive Write (CREW) PRAM; and the Concurrent Read, Concurrent Write (CRCW) PRAM. In the case of the CRCW PRAM, a further sub-classification applies, based on the conflict resolution used to arbitrate over concurrent writes.

The simplicity and generality of the PRAM model led to its wide acceptance as a research tool, especially for research into: the *concurrent access problem* of how to service concurrent requests without underlying hardware support; the *memory management problem* of how to layout data in order to minimise contention [31, 32]; and the *routing/interconnection problem* of minimising slow-down caused by the routing of data. Unfortunately, the cost model associated with the PRAM did not prove to be very useful in practice. It was unable to express the disparate costs associated with real machines, such as the difference between accessing local or remote memory. Several additions to the basic PRAM model were made over the years in attempts to fix the mismatch between the model and reality. These extensions included attempts to account for processor asynchrony [52], network latency and limited bandwidth [4] and topological locality [122, 129, 240]. A good survey of the basic PRAM model and its variants can be found in [116]. Despite these improvements, the basic PRAM model is still unable to generate accurate cost estimates for code running on real hardware platforms and it usefulness for performance prediction on actual parallel machines is of very limited scope.

Chapter 4

Hoare; Milner; Alur and Dill

There are several well known methods for the formal analysis of concurrency. Principal among these are Hoare's famous Communicating Sequential Processes (CSP) [125, 126, 201], proposed in 1978, and Milner's Calculus of Communicating Systems (CCS) [164] from 1980; both are closely related [37] and can be traced to Dijkstra's pioneering work on Cooperating Sequential Processes in 1968 [67]. CSP and CCS are often described as *process algebras*, because they provide a powerful mathematical framework for specifying the behaviour of parallel processes. However, brief perusal of any work on, for example, CSP will attest that "all of these dialects have been 'blackboard' languages: they have been used for describing parallel systems when the intended audience is human" [207] (although that cited work was aimed at making CSP definitions more amenable to mechanical analysis). The reason for this is connected with the way in which these formal methods are constructed.

Formal methods define a rigorous syntax and semantics for a small number of basic operators that describe sequential processing, parallel composition, synchronisation, communication, interruption and deterministic or non-deterministic choice. These operators can be used to create models of specific applications. These models are then evaluated for all possible sets of event sequences that could occur, typically with respect to some sort of acceptance condition for the purpose of model validation. Common acceptance conditions are the absence of deadlock or livelock, or constraint checking for model parameters. Essentially, the main purpose of most formal methods is to rigorously prove or disprove the correct operation of concurrent systems. In order to achieve this, every operational detail of a parallel system must be specified in great detail. Because of the complexity involved with this, both in terms of model construction and model evaluation, formal methods are mainly reserved for modelling concurrent systems where failure is not an option. For example, communication protocols are frequently verified for correctness using formal modelling techniques.

One of the main extensions to the original CSP definition was the inclusion of timing information [62, 63, 192, 209, 210], resulting in Timed CSP (TCSP). Obviously performance modelling would be impossible without this facility. The extensions are relatively straight-forward, and merely consist of annotating CSP operators with a deterministic quantity that represents the time required for the operation to complete. A further experimental addition to CSP resulted in Probabilistic Biased Timed CSP (PBTCSP) [150, 151], which allowed probabilistic models to be attached to the choice operator. However, these probabilistic choice operators only allowed binary decisions to be made based on two probabilities, which seems overly restrictive. Despite this simplification, proofs involving PBTCSP were described as rather complex; perhaps tellingly, PBTCSP models do not appear to have been described or applied elsewhere. Both the binary choice limitation of PBTCSP and the difficulty just described highlight the primary aim of all TCSP-based approaches. Despite the notion of time, TCSP-based approaches are obviously designed to prove the correct ordering of modelled events, rather than the time at which they occur; time is merely added to facilitate modelling of systems where time is inextricably linked with the ordering of events, such as timeouts in network protocols. Arguably, therefore, TCSP-based approaches are not truly intended for performance modelling of parallel systems, although in theory they could be used in such a way.

Conversely, similar work by Alur and Dill on a formal theory of timed automata [7] was fundamentally designed around the notion of time. Therefore, although their approach was also mainly intended for model-checking, it is arguably more applicable to the performance modelling of concurrent systems. Furthermore, and unusual for formal modelling systems, their approach can incorporate probabilistic timing delays with state transitions [6], which makes it particularly appropriate for realistic modelling of physical processes. Recently, some research has applied these general principles to the performance modelling of parallel processes [119].

Unfortunately, however, despite the accuracy and provable correctness that can be achieved with formal modelling tools, they are yet to be generally useful for the performance modelling of large-scale parallel programs. Currently, it is essentially impossible to translate many real-world problems – for example non-trivial message-passing parallel programs – into realistic formal models. Even if this could be achieved, these models generally take an exponential (in the size of the model) amount of time to solve, and any performance implications they uncover may be difficult to understand due to model complexity. In summary, formal methods are not currently able to effectively model the performance of large-scale parallel programs.

Chapter 5

Valiant

In 1990, Valiant [243] described a promising technique for writing efficient, portable parallel programs with predictable performance called Bulk Synchronous Parallelism (BSP). Valiant saw that one of the biggest problems with the message-passing approach was that deriving analytic cost models for performance prediction was very difficult because of the number and complexity of data transfers associated with it. Instead, the BSP methodology requires parallel programs to be structured so that their computation and communication are separated so that each can be considered as a bulk quantity. Because BSP considers communications *en masse* it is simpler to estimate bounds on communication time compared with unstructured message-passing. A good overview and comparison of BSP to other techniques can be found in [223].

Computation in BSP programs flows through a series of parallel *supersteps*, each of which is divided into three phases. In the first phase, each processor/memory pair P is involved in computation using only local data. This can be modelled by McColl's parameter s [157] which represents the number of basic operations (such as addition or multiplication) that can be carried out by a processor in one second. In the second phase, processes share data in a communication phase. During the communication phase, any number of messages can be sent and received. The communication pattern is defined by what is called an h-relation, which involves each process sending and receiving at most h messages. Usually, h is used as a compound parameter that also accounts for the total size in bytes of messages encountered by a process, m; i.e. hm is usually abbreviated to h. The communication time is modelled by the parameter g which represents the time required for an h-relation to complete under continuous message traffic between random processes. The parameter g is normally determined empirically for a particular machine, and is related to the machine's bisection bandwidth, the performance of the network stack, the buffer management used, the routing strategy and the BSP run-time system. In the final phase a barrier synchronisation is performed, where the duration of this synchronisation is modelled by the parameter l which is also determined empirically.

The execution time of a BSP superstep can be computed from the text of the program and the parameters of the target architecture which were described above. The *standard cost model* used to do this is:

$$superstep\ cost = max\{w_0, ..., w_i, ..., w_P\} + max\{h_0 g, ..., h_i g, ..., h_P g\} + l$$

where i ranges over the processes and w_i is the time for local computation at process i. Hence, subject to the constraints of predicting the run-time of serial programs (for example using techniques such as those of Knuth [139] or Dunning [73]) performance can be predicted. Inspecting the standard cost model, it is clear that efficient BSP programs must: balance the computation between processes to minimise w_i; balance the communication between processes to minimise $h_i g$; and minimise the number of supersteps to reduce the number of barrier synchronisations of duration l that are required.

Achieving these requirements for a specific program can be aided by tools from the BSPlib Toolset [124], which can create a performance description from trace data obtained by a once-only run of the code on any parallel machine. The performance model that is generated can be used in the design process for writing the BSP program, when porting the BSP program to new parallel computers, or when making purchasing decisions for a parallel computer (based on its s, g and l parameters). The BSPlib Toolset also provides some insight into the extent of performance improvements that could be made by using an asynchronous message-passing implementation such as the Message-Passing Interface (MPI) [102, 161, 162] or E-BSP [133], which extended the definition of the h-relation by adding notions of locality and unbalanced communication to the BSP model.

Chapter 6

Hockney

In 1991, Hockney introduced a model for describing asymptotic performance [127]. It was based on the maximum rate at which some activity can be performed (r_∞) and an associated value, based on a parameterisation of size, at which half the peak performance can be sustained ($n_{1/2}$). The original purpose of this model was to characterise performance on vector processors, where r_∞ represented the maximum rate of floating point operations that could be achieved, and $n_{1/2}$ represented the vector length for which half of that rate was actually achieved. More recently, this approach has been applied to characterise the performance of many systems. Notably, it is used when specifying a machine's performance on the Linpack benchmark [69] to rank the Top 500 fastest computers in the world [68]. More relevant to performance modelling, in a paper by Getov, Hockney and Hey [97], it was applied to distributed memory multicomputers. They showed that a machine could be empirically characterised by peak and half-performance parameters for a variety of small parcels of computation and communication. The performance of a program could then be predicted by counting its number and size of operations and summing their contributions to overall execution time. While this model is certainly useful for modelling simple, regular parallel programs, it suffers from two main problems in general. Firstly, it becomes intractable for complex parallel programs (at least without some form of automation), because it requires a large number of separate empirical models. Secondly, it does not provide particularly accurate models. Indeed, it simply provides a first order linear approximation to performance characteristics.

Chapter 7

Saavedra and Smith

A simple yet attractive approach to performance modelling was proposed by Saavedra and Smith in 1992 [203,204]; a very similar approach was also undertaken more recently by different authors [155]. Although neither method was not able to account for parallelism at all, it is possible that the general principles on which it operates could be applied to parallel programs. Saavedra and Smith's work noted that traditional benchmarking techniques alone fail to characterise programs and machines, hence results generated in such a way were tied to a specific program on a particular machine. They showed that a more general performance modelling system could be achieved with: a narrow-spectrum (micro) benchmarking tool [22] as a *machine characteriser* to determine the performance of abstract operations on a particular machine; a *program analyser* to statically count the number of those abstract operations in each basic block and dynamically count the order of those basic blocks during a trial run of an instrumented version of the program; and an "execution predictor", which could combine the results of the previous two stages and predict overall program performance. The one notable limitation of this technique is that it does require each program to actually be run at least once (and again where any different compiler optimisations are in play) prior to modelling, which limits its usefulness as a prototyping tool. To verify their approach, Saavedra and Smith used it to predict the Standard Performance Evaluation Corporation (SPEC) '89 [230] and Perfect Club [58] benchmark performance of several Reduced Instruction Set Computer (RISC) machines. In summary of those results, their simulations could quickly predict overall run-time to within 30% accuracy for 95% of cases. The difficulty of conducting accurate micro-benchmarking was listed as the major factor limiting overall modelling accuracy.

Clearly this general technique could be applied to the performance modelling of message-passing parallel programs if: 1) accurate micro-benchmarking of message-passing operations could be conducted; and 2) that any non-deterministic program execution as the result of variable message-passing performance could be accounted for.

Chapter 8

Culler *et al.*

In 1993 Culler *et al.* [56] noted that vast amounts of previous research had focused on overly detailed but flawed models of parallel computation, for example the PRAM which they considered unrealistic because it was synchronous and it assumed instantaneous interprocessor communication [228]. Furthermore, although the BSP model had attempted to bridge these limitations by allowing processors to communicate asynchronously and by accounting for memory latency and finite bandwidth availability, it did so at the cost of prescribing a restricted programming methodology.

Accordingly, Culler *et al.* developed a new model called LogP that is based on BSP but requires less enforced program structure and allows a programmer more control over their program. In contrast to the BSP model, the LogP model does not require a global barrier to separate communication and computation phases and it adds the notion of a finite network capacity that can only support a certain number of messages in transit at once. This makes LogP slightly more general than BSP, although the two models are able to efficiently simulate each other in most circumstances [23]. In other circumstances, LogP empowers programmers to take into account technology trends in order to improve the performance of their solution to a problem. In particular, Culler *et al.* realised that "technological forces [were] leading to massively parallel machines constructed from at most a few thousand nodes, each containing a powerful processor and substantial memory, interconnected by networks with limited bandwidth and significant latency." [56]. The LogP model uses four parameters that were designed to capture the effects of these factors. These are:

- *Computing bandwidth* supplied by the number of processors/memory units, P.

- *Communication bandwidth* between the processors $1/g$, where g represents the minimum gap between consecutive messages.

- *Communication latency* between processors, modelled as a constant L which represents the upper bound of the actual latency that may be observed by a short message when measured under unloaded conditions.

- *Coupling efficiency* between communication and computation, which is modelled by a parameter o that represents the overhead involved in message transmission.

Culler *et al.* [56] also suggested some general programming recommendations to guide efficient parallel algorithm design. Although these are not specifically related to the LogP model, they do highlight common parallel programming techniques that a performance model should be capable of accounting for:

- The *coordination of work assignment* [9, 247], which is concerned with how the processing that must be done should be divided up between available processors.

- The *coordination of data placement* [33,57], which is concerned with how the data that is required by individual processors should be distributed.

- The *provision of balanced communication* to make the best and most timely use of bandwidth availability.

- The *overlapping of communication with computation* because it is important to keep processors busy with useful work while waiting for data to arrive from remote processes.

Chapter 9

Grama *et al.*

Finding a good parallel algorithm to solve a given problem is usually very difficult because the efficiency of parallel algorithms is often very dependent on critical system parameters, such as the number of processors used, and the latency and bandwidth of the network that connects them. Therefore, scalability analyses are often done to determine how well particular algorithms perform, or scale, as the number of processors, interconnection speed or problem size are varied. One of the most common techniques for assessing scalability is to use an isoefficiency function, described by Grama *et al.* in 1993 [101]. The isoefficiency function of a parallel algorithm is an analytic expression that expresses the increase in problem size that is required to maintain efficiency as the number of processors assigned to a problem is increased. In order to find the isoefficiency function for a given algorithm, the efficiency E of the algorithm is first found by either direct measurement and subsequent curve fitting or complexity analysis (such as that found in [140]) and expressed as:

$$E = \frac{Speedup}{Number\ of\ processors} = \frac{1}{1 + \frac{T_o}{T_1}}$$

where T_o represents the parallel overhead as a function of problem size and number of processors used, and T_1 is the execution time of the algorithm on one processor. This expression is then transformed via algebraic manipulation to determine an isoefficiency expression for T_o that maintains constant efficiency for increasing numbers of processors.

Practically speaking, because of their simple nature, isoefficiency functions are not able to cope with non-linear sources of performance loss, such as load imbalance or contention. However, the isoefficiency function of an application with regular computation and communication can be used to predict the performance of that application for fixed-size problems on various numbers of processors, or on machines with different network characteristics (provided that these characteristics can be explicitly stated in the expression for T_o). In another form, the isoefficiency function of an algorithm can also be used to determine the size of a problem that can be solved by a given machine in a fixed time. Finally, the scalability of different algorithms can be contrasted by comparing their respective isoefficiency functions with respect to the number of processors used. Algorithms are said to be highly-scalable if the data size only needs to increase linearly with the number of processors used. Poorly scalable algorithms require the data size to be increased more rapidly in order to maintain constant efficiency.

Chapter 10

Adve

In 1993, Adve [1] submitted a dissertation that analysed the behaviour and performance of parallel programs. The model he presented was a significant step forward in the performance modelling of parallel programs because it provided far more qualitative and quantitative information about the performance of a parallel program than earlier methods had, but for comparable computational effort. While most of the models developed prior to Adve's model could only be applied to programs with simple synchronisation structures or required complex and heuristic solution techniques, his model could enable a programmer to relatively accurately predict the impact of underlying system changes as well as guide program design decisions for finding an effective, efficient parallel solution to a problem.

Adve's thesis developed and validated a deterministic model of parallel program performance prediction and testing its accuracy, efficiency, and practicality for real programs on realistic input data sets. The model used deterministic values for mean task times and communication times, while shared resource contention was computed from a separate, stochastic model. Combined with abstract representations for the separate behaviour of programs and systems, the model made it possible to analyse hypothetical programs and systems as well as combinations of these.

Although a fundamental limitation of Adve's model is that it cannot account for variance due to communication delays, his research showed that in reality, for many codes on many machines, the principal effect of random delays is to increase the mean execution time between synchronisation points and to leave the variance unaffected. This result contradicted a common assumption at that time that there was a large variance in parallel execution times. The key implication of Adve's thesis is that "it could be reasonable to ignore the variance of task and process execution times when computing synchronisation costs in a parallel program" [1].

In Adve's model, the total execution time was the sum of four components:

$$t_{total} = t_{computation} + t_{communication} + t_{resource\ contention} + t_{synchronisation}$$

where $t_{computation}$ excluded any computation performed when overlapped communication was occurring. While this model was conceptually simple, in practice it was non-trivial because of the non-deterministic nature of resource contention and because it can be extremely difficult to estimate average synchronisation delays.

Deriving model inputs is an important part of the modelling process. Adve's approach required two main inputs. The first was the task graph of the program. The second were the sets of resource usage parameters for individual tasks which were either deduced or measured by experiment. Constructing the task graph for a program is equivalent to reproducing the parallel control structure of the program. This can be achieved from a basic understanding of the program and carrying out little or none of its actual computation. Adve used a task graph to represent program behaviour because he believed that it is an appropriate level of abstraction for an analytical model. He defined:

- A *task* as the basic unit of work;

- A *task graph* as a directed acyclic graph that describes the inherent parallelism in a program, where nodes represent tasks and edges represent the relationships between tasks.

- A *process* as an entity that could be scheduled on a processor to execute tasks.

- A *condensed task graph* as a task graph, reduced so that each node denotes a collection of tasks that could be executed by a single process.

- A *fork-join task graph*, consisting of parallel phases of computation separated by full barrier synchronisations.

Construction of a condensed task graph reduces a graph so that each vertex represents the work performed between synchronisation points. Condensed task graphs can be orders of magnitude smaller than task graphs and are a useful construct for reducing complexity. A commonly occurring subclass of condensed task graphs are fork-join task graphs which are able to describe programs written in procedural languages. These fork-join task graphs have boundaries between synchronisation points and this helps to avoid a state-space explosion. A number of other models have been developed for reducing task graphs but these are likewise restricted, in particular, to the relatively simple but extremely common fork-join task graphs [10, 70, 241, 242, 249].

One troublesome problem of these approaches is that some programs have non-deterministic processing requirements, which can vary significantly between different executions of a program. This occurs in part because of the presence of data-dependent effects such as conditional branch probabilities or dynamic loop bounds. Although other techniques had been successfully used to model this using stochastic task execution times [10, 70, 135, 153, 154, 206], they were not compatible for incorporation with the deterministic task model used by Adve. Even so, Adve's technique remains applicable for a significant proportion of message-passing programs, with the added advantage that:

> "the deterministic assumption ... implies a unique execution sequence for the program, and furthermore [that] the delay at each synchronisation point in this sequence can be calculated as simply the numerical maximum of the execution times of the synchronising process." [1]

Chapter 11

Singh *et al.*

In 1994 Singh *et al.* [217] published a paper that examined the advantages of emerging methodologies over PRAMs. Singh *et al.* suggested that a useful parallel programming methodology must be abstract enough to be usable, detailed enough to capture fundamental properties, and general enough to run efficiently on different platforms without algorithmic changes. They argued that in order to achieve this, the modelling community needs to obtain a better understanding of the communication properties of parallel algorithms. Although several communication patterns such as dense linear algebra computations, computations on regular grids and fast Fourier transforms are determinable analytically, it is difficult to model the dynamic computations that are crucial in many real world applications such as computations on irregular grids (for example [20, 45, 61]), in Monte Carlo simulations, or in codes exhibiting adaptive parallelism (such as [39]). Still, they believed that even for these more complex algorithms, some form of characterisation of their communication properties should be possible.

A necessary input to performance models is a description of the communication properties of the program. Determining these properties is one of the most difficult parts of the modelling process. Singh *et al.* identified three sources of communication in a program:

- Inherent communication in the algorithm, i.e. the communication which would occur even if every processor had the entire dataset of the program in local memory.

- Communication resulting from finite local memory capacity.

- Communication from memory organisation effects.

This is instructive because it makes a distinction between local and remote data that a process must access. Furthermore, it highlights that there will be complex performance considerations even for local data depending on where the data reside in the storage hierarchy. In addition to these concerns, modelling of communication is made difficult by several other factors:

- Realistic data sets are often non-uniform over the input domain creating data-dependencies which make analysis difficult.

- Algorithm complexity can render even uniform domains difficult to model because of processing dependencies and interacting data structures.

- Some algorithms have a dynamically changing structure or utilise dynamic load balancing techniques [47, 61, 64, 149, 181, 216, 227].

Most models prior to the work of Singh *et al.* focused on the second and third factors identified above. The main contribution made by Singh *et al.* was the demonstration that characterising data sets is often just as important as characterising algorithms.

Chapter 12

Mehra *et al.*

In a 1994 paper, Mehra *et al.* [159] described how simulation could be a convenient tool for answering "what-if" questions during program design (see also [27, 194]) such as:

- What if the communication links were twice as fast?
- What if the CPU on each node could be sped up twofold?
- What would happen if one could have a machine with 8192 processors running a scaled-up problem?
- What if algorithm B was used instead of algorithm A?
- What if data were distributed across the processors differently?

They suggested several characteristics that a modelling technique should possess in order to answer such questions:

- *Generality*. A model should not be tied to a particular problem size, process mapping or system configuration and performance estimates should be easily adaptable to other platforms by substituting appropriate constants for the relative costs of computation and communication.

- *Accuracy*. A model should provide some quantitative measure as to its accuracy.

- *Rapid modelling*. It should be possible to create a model quickly without having to model minutiae.

At the lowest level, instruction level models have very accurate predictions but simulated runs take even longer than actual runs and they will not generalise to other platforms easily. Higher level models are more amenable to rapid modelling and can provide generality through abstractions that can model data distributions, interprocessor data movements and the like, but it is more difficult to quantify the accuracy of such models.

Mehra *et al.* [159] demonstrated that an effective way to represent a performance model at arbitrary levels of detail was to use a performance language. They found that the performance characteristics of Single Program, Multiple Data (SPMD) programs, which they noted form the majority of all message-passing programs, could be described with a performance language that supported syntactic constructs such as subroutines and loops so that repetitive behaviours could be expressed compactly. Furthermore, they were able to preserve procedure and block boundaries throughout the modelling process. Their modelling technique considered the order complexity of sequential blocks of code as well as dependency information for communication operations. This required a knowledge of the run-times of sequential blocks of code, the lengths and destinations of messages, and the extent of loop bounds. Obtaining this information from a program was a two-step process that involved the extraction of relevant information for parameter estimation from the program followed by formula discovery to fit parameterised equations to measured or hypothetical run-times.

An object-oriented "behaviour description language" was used to represent parallel programs as a collection of autonomous computing objects called players. These players had methods called key application subroutines that could be invoked by messages. Their model used the following constructs to model parallel programs:

- Sequential blocks of code were modelled using the statement (**Run** *duration*); which represented *duration* seconds of computation on a processor.

- Non-blocking send statements were modelled by the statement (**Post** *recipient message* : **length** *bytes*); where *recipient* represented the destination processor of a message containing the data *message* of length *bytes*.

- Blocking receives were modelled by the statement (**Receive** *message* [: **from** *sender*]); where *message* was the label of the data contained in the message and the optional *sender* parameter denoted the source of the message.

- Overheads such as buffer copying were simulated using the (**Hold** *duration*) statement which caused *duration* seconds of idling on the processor. In particular, message-passing delays were determined empirically and modelled using a (**Hold** *msgxmitdelay*) statement.

- Program control flow was modelled with the following C-like expressions:
  - (**BdlRoutine** *name* (*args*)(*variables*)*statement*+)
  - (**Repeat** *times statement*+)
  - (**If** *condition statement*+)
  - (**Branch** (*probability statement*+)...)

They developed a simulator called Axe which modelled multicomputers of homogeneous processing elements connected by a point-to-point network where each node had its own local memory, CPU and operating system kernel for message forwarding, task scheduling and memory management. Axe was sufficiently expressive to parameterise message-passing programs on distributed memory machines and was used to present a comparison of the profiled performance of two example programs with models that were generated for the same programs. The models were built by hand and required many man-months of effort but were very accurate. However, it was believed that the modelling procedure could be automated and investigations were subsequently begun into an automatic model generator [158].

Chapter 13

Parashar and Hariri

Parashar's 1994 PhD thesis [179] and a related paper authored with Hariri [180] described a novel, interpretive approach for making accurate and cost-effective predictions about the performance of parallel programs. In contrast to existing tools, which required either hand-crafted models or post processed run-time traces to enable performance visualisation and analysis, their techniques provided the means for purely compile-time performance estimation. This allowed the ramifications of decisions about problem decomposition, communication and synchronisation strategies to be far more easily explored. The three step process they described involved: 1) the creation of an abstract model of system hardware capabilities; 2) the creation of an abstract model of application structure; and 3) subsequent evaluation of the execution of the abstract application on the abstract system hardware.

System abstraction involved the manual hierarchical decomposition of a parallel machine's hardware into a system abstraction graph (SAG), where each node in the graph, or system abstraction unit (SAU), represented the performance characteristics of either a processing component, memory component, communication/synchronisation component or I/O component. In contrast, application abstraction was performed by an automatic compiler. Parashar and Hariri implemented a compiler for translating HPF or Fortran 90D programs into Fortran 77 plus message-passing programs, augmented with parametric information describing the performance behaviour of individual programming constructs called application abstraction units (AAU). In particular, they used

AAUs to signify sequential computation, process forking, iterative and conditional execution, communication and synchronisation. Iterative AAUs were subclassified into either deterministic, synchronised or non-deterministic varieties. If the compiler could statically decide that a loop had a fixed number of iterations and did not contain any communication or synchronisation calls, this would result in a deterministic AAU that linearly extrapolated the execution time of the sequential computation. The case where a loop contained communication or synchronisation operations would result in a series of interleaved deterministic AAUs and communication/synchronisation AAUs, which would be used to construct a recursively defined analytical performance expression. In the most general case of non-deterministic loop conditions, loop unrolling would evaluate each iteration separately. Conditional AAUs were similarly subclassified, using functional interpretation to resolve execution flow. Where variables affecting control flow could not be automatically determined, they would be tagged and the user would be asked to specify their value during the model evaluation phase. Finally, all AAUs would be combined into an application abstraction graph, defined by the execution structure of the program, with nodes representing computation events and edges representing communication and synchronisation events.

Given the resources defined by a parameterised SAU, an interpretation engine was designed to recurse over AAGs, evaluating the time required for each of its AAUs to execute (and timestamping those events), thereby predicting overall program performance. Estimation of the time required for each AAU to read or write various parts of the memory hierarchy used an approximation of access patterns based on global access and miss counts for each program variable as well as local block access counts and last used timestamps for each program variable, and the cache block size, associativity and replacement algorithm defined by the SAG. Communication and synchronisation performance was modelled using fixed latency and bandwidth parameters, plus the waiting time required to access communication links and buffers. The waiting time was modelled by a global communication structure, which maintained information such as the source, destination, and transmission time of each communication and synchronisation event. This information could theoretically be used by the interpretation engine to simulate the effects of access contention to shared network resources, given a sufficiently detailed SAG. However, it seems that this information was only intended to be used for roughly synchronising the simulated start/finish times of group communication. Indeed, this is confirmed by the existence of a global, user-defined factor $f_{overlap}$ in Parshar and Hariri's model, which must be empirically derived from performance measurements of a specific code, that weights the time required for communication AAUs to account for the overlapping of communication and computation. These facts suggest that the underlying network models used by Parshar and Hariri were not accurate enough to account for network contention nor the non-determinism to which they contribute.

Because of the parametric nature of SAGs, Parshar and Hariri's modelling system could easily predict the effects of different hardware platforms on program performance simply by re-evaluating AAGs for various parameter settings. The output module of the interpretation presents performance statistics, including a breakdown of computation time, communication time and wait time, as well as execution traces that can be viewed in Paragraph [117]. In [180], Parshar and Hariri provided an experimental validation of their modelling system using the NPAC HPF benchmark suite [165]. On tests using up to 8 processors, they managed to achieve prediction accuracy within 5% most of the time, and 20% in the worst case – the latter for higher numbers of processors. In addition, they used their system to make (unvalidated) predictions for larger configurations, and showed predicted results for 16 and 32 processor jobs, with varying processor speed and network load. Importantly, they showed how a hypothetical increase in network load would become extremely important for jobs utilising a large number of processors, clearly showing that very good network models will be required to obtain good performance predictions of programs run on large parallel machines.

Chapter 14

Skillicorn

In 1995, Skillicorn [219] identified three criteria that a parallel programming methodology must meet to be generally useful:

- *Architectural independence*. Since code is likely to be run on a wide variety of platforms, efficiency should not be tied to a particular architecture.

- *Congruency*. It is essential that the true cost of a program in terms of time and resources on the machine is reflected in the programming model.

- *Descriptive simplicity*. If software that is developed for a particular methodology is to outlast a specific architecture, it is crucial that it be built around a model that is sufficiently abstract.

Widely available libraries for message-passing such as MPI or the Parallel Virtual Machine (PVM) [92] have dealt successfully with the issues of architectural and platform independence (for instance, refer to Baker and Fox [18]) and descriptive simplicity, but congruency has not been adequately dealt with. Although message-passing inherently has the properties that make it a congruent methodology, this had not been specifically studied before Skillicorn's work and the property is still rarely used in practice. One of the contributions of Skillicorn's work was his systematic development of a theory and practice of congruency in message-passing programs.

Since the design of many programs is driven more or less by performance concerns, it is important for a programming methodology to have predictable costs. Run-time is usually the primary concern but others include development costs or resource costs. Cost measures are more difficult to analyse for parallel programs than sequential programs. The construction of cost measures for sequential programs is often divided into two phases: algorithm choice and fine tuning, since only the constants in front of asymptotic costs are affected. This means that the cost functions of serial software are usually composable and total cost is easily computable by summing the cost of its parts since it is convex; importantly, it is not possible to reduce the overall cost by increasing the cost of one part. In 1994, Skillicorn wrote more about the desirable properties of cost systems:

> "It is highly desirable to have the cost function defined in the same compositional way as the program semantics: A cost is associated with each basic operation, and rules are given to compute the cost of a composed program from the cost of its components". [218]

Given this goal, he went on to develop the idea of a *cost calculus* for the performance of parallel systems [222]. This is not simple for parallel systems because there are cost implications associated with rearranging operations. Because of this, such a calculus would require a calculational transformation system where the cost of a transformation could be calculated by a set of rules. Such a system could be made to work for any programming language for which deterministic costs could be obtained for the basic operations, even if they were in a parametric form.

Skillicorn argued that without this kind of composability it would be impractical to derive or optimise program performance in a modular way because implementation choices at some particular part of the program would necessitate a consideration of the cost implications for every other part of the program. Also, for this idea of composability to remain valid, Skillicorn noted that the decisions made by the compiler and run-time system must be reflected in the cost system, even though they may not be explicitly described by the programmer at implementation time. One way to build such a cost system would be to make the programming model low-level enough so that all of the decisions such as data decomposition, process placement and communication would need to be explicitly made by the programmer. Determining the cost of a program would then become an exercise in analysing program structure. Skillicorn acknowledged that MPI programs are amenable to such analysis in another paper also published in 1994, although in that paper he also alluded to shortcomings with the basic MPI program model:

> "The big problem with parallel computation today is finding the right level of abstraction. Machines and architectures change frequently. There is a need to develop software that can run on new machines with relatively little change. A good level of abstraction should be mathematically based. MPI makes it easy to build efficient implementations but does not help much with properties that programmers want." [220]

Although MPI does not always provide the features that programmers want, such as those provided by higher level languages such as High Performance Fortran (HPF), OpenMP, or other massively parallel systems [60], these properties can easily be (and often are) implemented on top of message-passing primitives [141]. Since message-passing can serve as the technological base for such features and many foreseeable developments in parallel programming methodologies (for example those that emerge with new technologies such as the Virtual Interface Architecture (VIA) [53]), this issue is not so important. Developing performance models of MPI primitives will automatically provide a performance model for these new methodologies.

Skillicorn also extended the algorithmic skeleton idea [38, 51] of using pre-structured building blocks for computation to the realm of communication skeletons [221]. Algorithmic skeletons encapsulate control structures such as frameworks for divide and conquer algorithms or task queueing systems. Each skeleton corresponds to a standard algorithm fragment which can be used as part of a larger program. The compiler or library writer chooses how each algorithm is implemented and how intra-skeleton and inter-skeleton parallelism can be exploited on the target architecture. This raises the level of abstraction considerably. It also means that the implementation of each building block needs to only be done once per architecture. A communication skeleton is an interleaving of computation steps and fixed patterns of communication on an abstract topology. Communication skeletons are efficiently implementable and can have defined cost measures. It allows building blocks to be internally parallel but composable sequentially so programmers do not need to be aware of parallel programming pitfalls. A real world example of this philosophy is ScaLAPACK [46], which combines a set of basic communication subroutines [253] and linear algebra subroutines [24] to create a package of parallelised linear algebra subroutines.

Chapter 15

Crovella and LeBlanc

In 1994 Crovella and LeBlanc [54, 55] presented a novel approach to the performance estimation problem called *lost cycles analysis* which distinguished between productive computation and parallel overhead. They reasoned that if they could predict the total performance lost to overhead in a parallel program and then subtract this from the peak performance that it is possible for the machine to reach, they would be able to predict the overall performance of a parallel program.

Although this may seem a convoluted way of predicting performance, it was not so strange after all, since if one knows the characteristics of a machine, its peak performance is trivial to calculate. Furthermore, predicting the performance degradation induced by the individual sources of overhead in a parallel program simplified the overall performance prediction problem by explicitly separating those effects that had a bearing on performance.

The model they designed was carefully crafted to be *complete* so that it captured all possible sources of overhead, as well as *orthogonal* so that the sources of overhead were mutually exclusive. Completeness is critical but it is often ignored in performance modelling tools, usually due to a focus on particular metrics such as cache-hit ratios or message traffic. Although such a focus would be useful if it corresponded to a dominant source of overhead, in reality, performance is often dominated by unexpected effects. Together, the properties of completeness and orthogonality ensured that their system could correctly calculate lost cycles and hence, indirectly determine pure computation.

In practice, the lost cycles approach used a tool to measure the sources of overhead in a program and another tool to fit the measurements that were made to analytic forms. A tool called *pp* measured parallel overhead by processing simple event logs that had been collected at run-time by using a logging library. A tool called *lca* was used to guide the user through the selection of a model to fit the output data from *pp* to analytic forms.

All categories of overhead were measured using the unifying metric *lost cycles*, an aggregate in seconds of parallel overhead. An advantage of the lost cycles approach was that it allowed quantitative study of the trade-offs between effects often modelled in incompatible ways. The categories of performance loss that were measured were:

- *Load imbalance* where any idle processor cycles occurred while unfinished parallel work existed.

- *Insufficient parallelism* for any idle processor cycles that occurred while no unfinished parallel work existed.

- *Synchronisation loss* for cycles that were spent acquiring a lock or waiting for a barrier synchronisation to complete.

- *Communication loss* for cycles that were spent waiting for messages to arrive from remote processes.

- *Resource contention* for cycles that were spent waiting for access to a shared hardware resource.

A small number of measurements for each effect was sufficient to parameterise an example model and lead to an aggregate model spanning the entire parameter space. The model was useful under varying conditions and crossover boundaries where one programming technique outperformed another were able to be obtained by solving simultaneous equations.

Chapter 16

Mraz; Tabe *et al.*

Variation in communication time, often called jitter, is a well-known phenomenon in telecommunication networks. However, studies by Mraz [168] in 1994 and Tabe *et al.* [236] in 1995 seem to be the only substantive investigations into the variance of communication time on parallel computers. The dearth of studies on this topic is probably because highly accurate clocks have not been generally available for most parallel computers in the past, which makes it impossible to time individual message-passing operations, and hence obtain distributions of message-passing performance. Therefore, most benchmarking efforts have focussed on average communication time over a large number of communications. Mraz and Tabe's studies of message-passing variance were possible, however, because their investigations focussed on the high-end IBM SP2 running AIX, which does provide a high resolution globally synchronised clock.

It is important to minimise jitter in real-time systems to maintain a steady flow of information. For example, too much jitter creates pop sounds in audio signals or jerkiness in video signals. Some parallel programs provide real-time output, and in these cases it is obviously important to minimise jitter. More problematic for parallel programs in general, however, is the detrimental effect of jitter on performance. If message delivery to one process of a parallel system is slow, that delay, to some extent, will eventually propagate through to every other process. In the worst case, every other process will sit idle, waiting for the delayed process to catch up. The chances of one process suffering late message delivery increases at least proportionately with the number of processes involved, but usually even more so due to increased contention. Further the performance degradation of a delayed message also increases in proportion with the number of processes. Unfortunately, therefore, while this effect may be negligible for parallel programs running on a small number of processors, it has the potential to severely limit performance when a larger number of processors are used. In fact, at some point, overall performance will begin to reduce as more processors are assigned to a problem; and beyond even that, another point will be reached where overall performance will become slower than if only one processor were used.

Mraz developed a "hot-potato" benchmark that measured the time to pass a virtual token around a ring of processors. Although, strictly speaking, this did not measure individual communication times, the number of processors in the ring was relatively small (2 to 64 in different cases) compared to the large number of repetitions used in other benchmarks to obtain average times (typically many thousands), so fine-grained timing characteristics did not become completely washed out. One noteworthy limitation of Mraz's approach is that he assumed that the time a message spent actually traversing the interconnection network was constant. Although in the case of his benchmark this would have been essentially true, because only one message could ever traverse the network at any given time (ignoring operating system traffic), it does not hold true in general: contention will introduce even more variance. Despite this he obtained some very interesting results. Mraz conducted 100,000 point-to-point communication tests using various message and ring sizes, and recorded the best, average and worst completion times observed, as well as a histogram of results for one test. His results showed that the average and minimum times were of the same magnitude, while the maximum times were up to two orders of magnitude larger. Closer examination of the histogram revealed that the bulk of the measurements formed an exponential-type distribution that tailed off within several multiples of the message latency, while a small but appreciable number of results accounted for the outlying events. Despite the significant variance of the delays, which in themselves would severely affect parallel program performance on a large numbers of processors, Mraz largely disregarded the main (i.e. exponential) part of the distribution in favour of analysing the outliers. By timing the iterations of a busy loop and correlating the results with the message-passing times that were observed, he deduced that the long delays corresponding to his outlying observations were due to operating system interruptions. The most significant of these was the operating system's process scheduler, which ran for 30-40 μs every 10ms. Other interruptions he was able to identify were due to the parallel program environment and page faulting. This insight was used to improve the AIX operating system by ganging common interrupts across all processors simultaneously, thereby removing the effect of unsynchronised stalls.

Tabe *et al*'s work extended Mraz's study by quantitatively investigating the effect of the very slow, outlying message-passing times on an all-to-all communication pattern. In particular, Tabe *et al* used a simulator to show how the performance variance of point-to-point message-passing introduced load imbalance on a microscopic scale, which, when summed over all communication operations, caused macroscopic performance degradation. This was validated against actual measurements of all-to-all performance, for the first time providing reasonable proof of why collective communication performance does not live up to expectations based on simple (constant) point-to-point microbenchmark performance.

Two other studies have also briefly mentioned the variance in message-passing communication times. Georgitsis [95, 96] observed that the distributions measured in Mraz's work could well be Poisson distributions, although no quantitative verification of this statement was provided. More recently, in a study on the architectural requirements of NASA's NAS Parallel Benchmarks (NPB) [17], Wong *et al.* [254] noted that the actual distribution of times observed in low-level message-passing on heavily loaded commodity networks did not correlate at all well with typical microbenchmark performance. For their machine, they found that while the return trip time measured by common microbenchmarking tools was only 50 μs, the mean time actually observed was 5ms with a similar variance.

Chapter 17

Clement, Quinn and Steed

An interesting approach aimed at dealing with the performance variability of parallel programs was presented by Clement and Quinn [48, 49]. They believed that because the low-level operations in a parallel program could take different lengths of time to complete, for example due to contention, the performance of those low-level operations should be modelled by stochastic values. Rather than trying to measure those values directly, their approach centred around inferring them from an analysis of program structure as well as measurements of overall program performance. The first stage of this process required a static program analysis tool to count the number of low-level operations in each basic block and a (dynamic) instrumentation run to determine the execution frequency of each basic block. In the second stage, this information would be mechanically converted into a (long) analytic expression parameterised by the performance of each low-level operation and input into a standard symbolic manipulation package. Finally, given a number of assumptions, they showed how multivariate data analyses could be used to discern the mean, variance and confidence interval for the performance of each low-level operation. The important assumptions were that: the performance parameters could be well-approximated by normal distributions with constant variances under all circumstances; the program comprised of a deterministic task structure, and especially that the number of loop iterations and the shape of data structures scaled linearly with problem size; communication performance could be well-approximated by a linear model based on message size; and that all models remained invariant across machine/compiler pairs. If all of these assumptions could be met, a program's performance sensitivity to critical system parameters such as message latency or bandwidth could easily be estimated by perturbing the inferred parameter values and re-evaluating the analytical performance expression. As an obvious extension to this, different (even hypothetical) values for the performance of low-level operations could be used to estimate the performance that could be achieved for the application on various parallel machines.

Although this approach was originally designed to cope only with regular communication in data parallel languages, it was later extended by Clement and Steed to deal with arbitrary PVM programs, and incarnated in a tool called APACHE [50, 231]. In this revised approach, they also introduced a simple means to roughly account for contention in shared networks (such as non-switched Ethernet) which involved augmenting the standard linear model of communication time T with a contention factor γ:

$$T = l + \frac{b\gamma}{W}$$

where l is link latency in seconds, b is the size of the message in bytes and W is the bandwidth of the link in bytes per second. Although, in general, γ could vary for every message, the APACHE model does not retain enough information to account for this, so γ must be assumed to be constant and equal to the number of processes. Consequently, a restriction of this model is that it assumes that all processes communicate simultaneously, which is only even roughly true for problems exhibiting regular computation and communication patterns. In several example cases where this assumption was shown to hold, however, Clement and Steed found the simple contention model greatly enhanced the accuracy of their performance predictions for essentially zero extra effort. For up to 8 processors on each of three different parallel machines, they found that APACHE was able to model the performance of Jacobi iteration to within 10% accuracy and matrix multiplication to within 30% accuracy. Prediction accuracy using more processors or on codes with less regular computation and communication patterns would presumably suffer because of APACHE's inability to predict the effects of non-linear performance factors.

Chapter 18

Islam

In a book published in 1995 [130] there is a useful chapter by Islam on *Characterising Parallel and Distributed Applications*. In it he explained that a parallel code has static attributes which are explicitly defined by the programmer, as well as dynamic attributes which can vary from one run of the program to another, even on the same machine.

Even though many dynamic events occur during a parallel program's execution, the processes of a parallel computation generally synchronise the execution of various parts of their own computations with subcomputations of other processes. The result of this is that common process interaction patterns between communication and computation phases can be identified. This is often referred to as a communication pattern. Of course, for any particular program there are dynamic attributes such as message size or iteration time that determine a unique version of the pattern. Typically, an application consists of a series of basic patterns, which Islam identified as:

- *Asynchronous* process interaction patterns with no explicit dependencies between processes.

- *Synchronous* process interaction patterns with explicit synchronisation points at the end of each phase of computation. This commonly occurring pattern is often found in iterative phases of SPMD programs, for which synchronisation occurs at the end of a loop.

- *Pipelined* patterns, either synchronous or asynchronous, where data flow through a process in a predefined order.

- *Client-server* and the related *bag-of-tasks* patterns where client processes compute results and communicate these with several servers or a single server, respectively.

These very standard process interaction patterns are often built on top of a message-passing paradigm using the following primitives:

- *Synchronous sends and receives* where both the sending and receiving processes block until they have completed successfully.

- *Asynchronous sends* where the sending process returns control immediately to the current thread of control and a separate thread is started to deal with the outgoing message. Similarly *asynchronous receives* do not block and wait for incoming data but must be used in conjunction with a polling method that determines when a message has arrived.

- *Exchange* calls where two processes send and receive data simultaneously.

- *Request-response* calls where a message is sent by a process that initiates processing on a remote process and a response is returned.

- *Multicast* and *broadcast* calls where a message is sent to some or all of the processes of an application respectively.

- *Reduction* where one process recombines messages from many sources at one destination.

Although it is possible to view all communication patterns as a collection of sends and receives, and they are usually implemented this way at low levels, aggregation into higher level patterns can provide a better characterisation for modelling purposes.

Chapter 19

Jonkers

In October 1995 Jonkers published his PhD thesis [131] which presented a new modelling formalism and associated software tools for the efficient performance prediction of parallel programs called GLAMIS (GeneraLised Architecture Modelling wIth Stochastic techniques).

To put his approach into perspective, he categorised the ways in which parallel program performance could be evaluated into three broad groups, namely *measurement, simulation* and *analytical techniques*. Measurement is only of very limited use during the initial stages of program design and implementation because it forces a measure-then-modify programming cycle which is very labour intensive. In some cases it is not even possible to measure program performance in the early stages of program design because the hardware is not available. Simulation is a more flexible option and can be used when the hardware is not available. It is also more suited to parameter studies although the results of a simulation are numerical and a separate evaluation is required for each set of input parameters. This can be computationally very expensive. Analytical techniques provide the most useful approach in the early stages of program development. Either numeric or symbolic models can be created, usually involving a trade-off between accuracy and flexibility. Numeric approaches are similar to simulation and usually more accurate, but symbolic models have far more scope for providing performance estimates under a wide range of conditions. This is useful in the early stages of program development because it can enable a programmer to find the best solution to a problem. Jonkers classified analytical performance modelling techniques according to their:

- *Expressive power* which is concerned with the ability of a model to describe the performance characteristics of a program and the machine it is running on.

- *Prediction accuracy*, where there are two sorts of errors that can be incurred. Firstly, there are inherent modelling errors because models are a simplification of reality and secondly, analytical errors which occur where small modelling inaccuracies are tolerated in order to make the models analytically tractable.

- *Robustness* which refers to the reliability of the predictions that are given by a performance model. This is often in the form of a sensitivity analysis to identify the situations that may lead to high prediction errors.

- *Analytical complexity*, in particular, the computing resources that will be required for computing a prediction and how long it will take to get that prediction.

- *Scalability* through the utilisation of replication constructs to allow the specification of machines with high degrees of symmetry. Large machines are often highly symmetric and model constructs for replication can improve comprehensibility and decrease analytical complexity.

- *Ease and comprehensibility* of modelling, especially in large and complex systems.

Jonkers chose to use a formal modelling language that allowed for the explicit specification of parallelism because it provided the most expressive power for an analytical modelling technique. It allowed a unified description of both parallel architecture models and program models to be constructed. Within this modelling framework, Jonkers described two general sources of performance loss. The first of these is called *condition synchronisation*. In the static form, which is familiar from normal serial computing, this is also known as a *precedence relationship* and it is implicit in the structure of the program. In parallel programs a dynamic form exists and it is associated with communication between cooperating processes. The second source of performance loss is *mutual exclusion* which is inherently dynamic. This can occur both at the machine level where it is called *resource contention* and at the program level where it is referred to as *critical sections*. Mutual exclusion is one of the most noticeable sources of non-determinism in parallel programs.

Because precedence relations are static, both deterministic and stochastic task times can be naturally modelled using task graphs, although complications arise due to conditional execution. In deterministic models, all quantities such as timing parameters and loop bounds need to be constant or at least representable in a symbolic fashion. In probabilistic models, some degree of uncertainty exists in timing parameters and stochastic quantities are used in the model. Many of the parameters that need to be modelled in a real system are nearly deterministic. For example, there is usually very little variation in time needed for a floating point operation. At a program level, numerical applications often use fixed loop bounds, for example to iterate over the number of columns in a matrix. Message-passing, however, is more problematic. It is dynamic and it cannot be modelled with task graphs unless communication times are assumed to be deterministic. Worse, mutual exclusion is inherently non-deterministic and cannot be modelled using task graphs at all.

Jonkers adopted a hybrid approach that used task graphs to express condition synchronisation and queueing networks to express mutual exclusion. This allowed both the machine and program to be described in a natural, comprehensible way. He devised an algorithm for the analysis of program models represented by general task graphs under the assumption of deterministic task completion times. This considerably simplified his analysis compared with purely stochastic approaches but still yielded very accurate predictions for a wide range of parallel applications.

In GLAMIS, Jonkers represented tasks dependencies with *Simple* (or *series parallel*) graphs. He did this because they could describe most commonly occurring message-passing programs and they were relatively simple to solve. For deterministic series parallel graphs, the total execution time could be deduced simply by using a critical path algorithm. A number of tasks in series could be replaced by one task with a delay equal to the sum of the delays, and a number of tasks in parallel could be replaced by a task with a delay equal to the maximum delay of the parallel tasks. Although Jonkers was focused on deterministic models, the previous work of Gelenbe and Liu [93] had shown that stochastic models were still feasible. In those models Gelenbe and Liu had obtained the overall distribution for parallel constructs by multiplying the constituent distributions and the overall distribution for series constructs by convolution.

Although Jonkers assumed task times to be deterministic in GLAMIS, service times for the queueing model representing the machine were probabilistic. Parallel architectures were modelled as virtual machines using a logical instruction set. Each of the instructions was parameterised and modelled by a queueing centre. The virtual machine instructions he used were floating point instructions, memory loads and stores, as well as message-passing primitives such as sends and receives. Programs were modelled using a sequence of series-parallel sections using a directed acyclic graph. The annotation of nodes in a task graph included an instruction count of the average number of times each instruction type is called in that task. Mapping from instructions to visit counts, which defined the queue structure, was machine-dependent. This machine model was formally defined using the tuple $<Q, S, Y, M, \delta, I, F>$. Q represented the queueing model elements with mean service time S, queue type Y, relative speedup δ and number of equivalent queueing centres M where replication was involved. I represented the logical instruction set of the machine and the function F was used to map instructions to visit counts.

One of the drawbacks of Jonkers' technique is that model construction involves significant manual effort, especially while building machine models. Regarding program models, Jonkers believed that construction could be partly automated using the by-products of parallelising compilers.

Chapter 20

van Gemund

In 1996, van Gemund described the performance modelling of parallel systems [244]. He attributed the difficulty in modelling parallel processes to the role that synchronisation plays in parallel systems. Like Jonkers, he divided this synchronisation into a static component and a dynamic component. The static component, known as condition synchronisation, occurs because of the precedence relationships between tasks. The dynamic component is caused by mutual exclusion which is due to resource contention at the machine level and critical sections at the program level. Van Gemund extended the scope of Jonkers' work to include the effects of conditional control flow, which also alters the dynamic nature of a program. The dynamic forms of synchronisation and conditional control flow lead to non-determinism which is very computationally expensive to model accurately. Accurate modelling involves solving a problem where the solution complexity grows with exponential order compared to the size of the system. This is because it requires evaluation of all the combinations of event orderings that can occur in the problem. As background for his work, van Gemund classified existing parallel program performance modelling techniques according to their ability to model synchronisation and conditional computation. Brief summaries of these approaches follow.

Deterministic graphs are a popular choice for modelling condition synchronisation in parallel programs because they have a very low solution cost. The crucial abstraction is performed during the modelling step which extracts a graph representing the inherent parallelism in a code from the program text.

After this, the technique yields to an exact analysis and execution time can be determined using a critical path algorithm. Unfortunately, these graphs cannot model mutual exclusion or conditional control flow which limits their predictive capability.

Stochastic graphs are an extension of the deterministic graph concept. Stochastic rather than deterministic values are used to represent task times by annotating graph edges with distributions that approximate the effect of conditional control flow and mutual exclusion (see Tayyab [239] and Yazici [257] for examples). Unfortunately, while it is relatively easy to determine average execution time from such graphs, determining the distribution of run-times that will be observed is very difficult unless restrictive assumptions are made [94, 146]. Instead, some approaches have investigated the simpler problem of determining performance bounds [74, 146].

Queueing networks can model mutual exclusion between contesting processes by using queueing centres to simulate the delays associated with access to a shared resource. For example, message-passing delays can be approximated by setting the mean service demand and service times at queueing centres based on the number of messages in transit and minimum message latencies. Such networks are usually solved for an average case using steady-state analysis. Often, exponentially distributed service times are assumed (citing a justification offered by Salza [205]) since this allows the queueing networks to be mapped to Markov chains. This is advantageous because such models can be solved using Mean Value Analysis (MVA) [191, 195] which allows an exact solution in polynomial time. Unfortunately, this assumption places unrealistic restrictions on the structure of code that it can model effectively [131]. Furthermore, although queueing networks can be good at estimating the delays in single phases of a parallel program, they are not able to model condition synchronisation. Because of this, they have been combined with task graphs to form hybrid models [131], resulting in a model that is essentially equivalent to a stochastic graph.

Petri nets (see Breanl [34] or Murata [169] for an overview of their properties) have more modelling power than task graphs or queueing networks and they can accurately model parallel systems [12, 136]. In fact, the closely related *extended petri nets* are as powerful as a Turing machine and theoretically they can describe any program written in any programming language. In the case of performance models, timed petri nets represent the time of basic operations with a transition time at each node of the network, condition synchronisation in the structure of the network, and mutual exclusion by using a non-determinism operator. In the case of a message-passing parallel program, a petri net model is normally constructed by separately modelling the blocks of computation between two consecutive communication statements. These submodels are then merged using rules that model communication among the processes. Although petri nets are very powerful, they have exponential solution complexity and are prohibitively expensive to solve for models of parallel programs of practical size. Furthermore, models of large programs become difficult to comprehend and aid programmers very little in understanding performance implications of algorithm choice during program design.

Simulation languages allow for arbitrarily high levels of modelling detail which gives them the potential to be most similar to the actual system. Simulation languages naturally account for condition synchronisation and mutual exclusion. Data-dependent control flow can be supported although this is often in a probabilistic context using weighted model parameters. Deriving performance estimates from simulation has the advantage over directly measuring actual systems because it is non-invasive and can even be done for hypothetical machines. Unfortunately, simulation languages are typically numerical rather than analytical in nature, which restricts the insight they can provide for performance optimisation.

Analytical modelling techniques (such as CSP and CCS from Section 4, APACHE from Section 17, PEL [146], TCAS [190] and others [15,19,59]) have an underlying calculus that can be used to describe the performance of a code. Successive approximations are used that produce less accurate but simpler models and ultimately, a performance model is expressed as a system of equations that retains parameters of interest. The advantage of this is that a model could then be used to easily investigate the performance implications of different parameter choices [48]. For example, Mendes *et al.* [160] produced a symbolic model for a code in terms of its problem size, the number of processors used, and a number of system parameters that were evaluated via benchmarking.

None of the analytical approaches before that of van Gemund's accounted for mutual exclusion. Van Gemund developed an analytical technique with a mathematical framework and calculus for approximating the performance of parallel systems aimed primarily at the initial phases of program design where extremely low solution cost rather than high accuracy is important. Techniques with low solution cost are of vital importance in initial design phases in order to study the performance implications of design choices through exploration of large parameter spaces. Van Gemund described a static approximation to the effects of mutual exclusion using his structured PerformAnce ModEling LAnguage (PAMELA) which defined a symbolic calculus for describing synchronisation. This calculus provided a set of approximation rules that, when repeatedly applied, reduced a model to an analytical expression in the time domain where machine and program parameters of interest were symbolically retained in the final time domain performance model. This allowed the computation of a deterministic time domain result that could be easily evaluated for different input parameters. This relied on several restrictions (in particular it assumed individual task times to be deterministic, based on previous work by Adve [1, 2]) to support low-cost, statically determinable models that had robust accuracy across entire parameter spaces. Examples of similar techniques can be found in a number of studies [77–81, 111, 245].

PAMELA evaluated performance models using critical path analysis for condition synchronisation and bounds analysis to approximate mutual exclusion. It used the same syntax to describe programs and machines which allowed a unified description of mutual exclusion at both the program and machine level. Van Gemund called the combination of critical path analysis and bounds analysis *serialisation analysis* since it was based on identifying the potential serialisation of contending model parameters. In addition, the symbolic nature of his analysis process allowed the effects of conditional control flow to be retained in the final performance model. The constructs that PAMELA used to model condition synchronisation, mutual exclusion and conditional control flow are summarised below.

Condition synchronisation was modelled in two ways. Condition synchronisation that was implicit in the structure of a program code was modelled using the sequential operator ";" and the parallel operator "||". Explicit condition synchronisation could be used to expressed using $wait\{c_1, c_2, c_3...\}$ and $signal(c_1)$ directives, which acted on conditions C_i. *Mutual exclusion* was supported at two levels of accuracy. At an exact level, achieved using numerical simulation, PAMELA supported the P/V construct of Dijkstra [66]. Van Gemund also defined a PAMELA construct to approximate mutual exclusion where access to resources (such as memory banks or processor scheduling slots) was controlled by *use* constructs. He defined $use(U, \tau) = P(U); delay(\tau); V(U)$ where U represented a set of resources. From this definition he developed a series of equations for calculating the delays caused by *use* statements in the time domain.

PAMELA provided an interesting solution for a fundamental problem of analytic prediction: static un-decidability due to data-dependent program parameters. *Conditional control flow* was partially supported by symbolic parameter retention. For example, consider the conditional operator $if(p)\ L$ where p is the probability of running the code L. In the final model the parameter p would be retained, which could then be specified by human intervention, or the model could be subjected to analysis given various p's. Another example of this is the $while(c)\ L$ loop where c is the loop condition and L is the loop code. Here, the unbounded while loop would be modelled as a loop bounded by a user specified parameter c. In other cases, van Gemund showed that it was possible to derive valid performance models of a program despite data-dependent execution since it is often known how much work needs to be done, even if the exact order in which it is computed is not known.

Calibration was not supported by PAMELA although van Gemund recognised its importance. Some analytical approaches feature calibration where certain parameters are determined by direct measurement of calibration routines rather than by calculation [90, 147]. A similar example of this can be found in a paper by Gupta and Banerjee [111] where communication cost was estimated in terms of an MPI-like abstract kernel of high level instructions.

In general, the execution time of code modelled using PAMELA should be stochastic with a finite distribution between a lower bound T^l and upper bound T^u. However, calculation of these distributions, even given the assumption of deterministic task times is a very complicated task and was not tackled by van Gemund in his dissertation. Instead, he chose to approximate these distributions by their lower and upper bounds. He developed exact solutions for the lower bound of run-time, T^l. Developing an exact bound for T^u proved to very complicated. Instead he derived equations for the upper bound of a distribution that was correct to within an unknown factor less than 2, which depended on specific circumstances. This was not a major concern, however, since he also showed that the vast majority of systems had a T^{mean} much closer to T^l than to T^u anyway.

Chapter 21

Labarta and Girona *et al.*

One of the most mature tools for predicting and visualising the performance of message-passing programs is Dimemas, which was conceived by Labarta and Girona *et al.* and described in their 1996 paper [144]. Dimemas simulates the time behaviour of a message-passing program using a trace file of its computation and communication structure and some simple parameters describing a target machine. For MPI programs, Dimemas uses trace files generated by linking a program with the VampirTrace [175] instrumented MPI library and running the resultant code on an existing parallel machine. Any parallel machine can be used for this instrumentation run - even a uniprocessor workstation running a number parallel processes in a time-shared fashion. Dimemas analyses the trace file based on elapsed CPU time measurements rather than wall-clock measurements for each process, and automatically adjusts the trace file to remove the time spent on unrelated processes. This introduces non-linear errors, for example by ignoring the effect of cache flushing as processes are swapped in and out, but a paper by Girona and Labarta [98] argued that the overall accuracy of the technique remains reasonable in many cases. A more fundamental limitation of Dimemas, however, is its inability to model non-determinism. Because the trace file is immutable, determined by the order of events during the instrumentation run, applications where the number and sequence of computations and communications depends on timing cannot be accurately modelled using Dimemas.

The target architecture supported by Dimemas is a network of SMP nodes, each with their own local memory and one or more processors. Processors are connected by multiple levels of bus-based communication links. Point-to-point communication performance is computed using a simple linear performance model, which can be roughly determined from the trace file or explicitly specified, augmented by a simple principle to roughly account for dynamic (non-linear) network contention: only one message may traverse a given bus at a time. More specifically, if there are m messages ready for transit but only b available buses then the messages are serialised into $\lceil m/b \rceil$ waves. This constitutes a first order approximation to contention, which is inherently non-linear.

For collective operations, a fan-in/fan-out model based on point-to-point communication is used [99]. The time required for the fan-in stage of a collective communication is modelled by:

$$T_{fan-in} = \left(l + \frac{s}{w}\right) * model\_in\_factor$$

where l is the link latency, s is the size of the data to operate on, w is the link bandwidth and *model_in_factor* is used to describe the number of steps in the collective algorithm. The expression for the time required during the fan-out stage of a collective algorithm is identical, except that "in" is replaced with "out". The *model_in/out_factor*s for any particular collective routine can be specified by the user, although a number of sensible defaults exist. Typical *model_in/out_factor*s are *constant*-, *linear*- or log_2-based functions, parameterised by number of processors. It is worth noting that this model assumes an implicit barrier so that all collective operations start at the same time. While this greatly simplifies the model, it comes at the cost of ignoring the effect of staggered starts on collective performance, which is common, especially in irregular programs.

Given a trace file of a program and the architectural parameters of a target platform, Dimemas performs a critical path analysis. It reports summary statistics such as total CPU usage for different code blocks and their importance for overall program execution time. It also produces output traces that can be viewed as space-time diagrams using Vampir [175]. Because the architectural parameters can be changed and the performance model re-run, Dimemas also allows a user to easily analyse a program's performance sensitivity to factors such as network latency or bandwidth. All of this information can be used to study load imbalances and potential parallelism, and ultimately predict the benefits of particular code optimisations.

Chapter 22

Dunlop and Hey *et al.*

In 1997, Dunlop and Hey showed that using instruction counting to model serial performance and simple ping-pong results to model communication performance fails to account for the memory hierarchy and can lead to a very significant mis-estimation of performance [121]. While it is well appreciated that cache behaviour plays a significant role in most serial codes [118], its effects are often neglected when predicting the behaviour and performance of parallel programs [121]. A possible reason for this is that cache behaviour is critically dependent on memory access patterns, hence a good model of cache behaviour can only be obtained by exactly simulating every single memory access. This is tremendously expensive; simulating the cache behaviour of a program will be far slower than actually running that program. Despite this, it can be very worthwhile to model and tune the cache behaviour of serial code because of the enormous performance improvements to which it may lead. Unfortunately, modelling the cache behaviour of parallel code is far more problematic. Obviously, there will be many processors to model, which makes cache simulation even slower. Far worse, though, are the effects that process scheduling and non-determinism – which are exponentially greater for parallel programs – can have on cache behaviour. Unlike the execution of serial code, where interruptions almost always lead only to transient anomalies in cache behaviour, the slightest change in the execution structure of some parallel codes can lead to radically different cache behaviour. Solving each of these behaviours is completely intractable. Despite this, however, it should still be possible to individually model the cache behaviour of the serial/computational parts of a parallel program in many cases. Strangely, however, very few modelling systems for parallel programs seem to take advantage of this reprieve.

In order to fill the void of performance estimation tools for parallel programs that take into account the memory hierarchy, Dunlop and Hey developed a Performance EstimatoR FOr RISC Microprocessors (PERFORM) [71, 72]. PERFORM uses execution-driven simulation to run the control framework of serial sections of code, taking into account any variables that may affect control flow. In addition, PERFORM relies on several simple but effective heuristics to avoid having to execute the entire control structure of a code, yet takes care to maintain reasonable accuracy. These mainly involve avoiding the need to simulate every loop iteration. For example, one heuristic is to only simulate a small number of loop iterations, check whether the completion time for each repetition has reached a steady state, and if so then use extrapolation to approximate the time required for all remaining iterations. Putting these optimisations aside, the time required to execute a serial section is computed by summing the time required to execute any data movement, computation or library calls that it encompasses. The time required for data movement - either explicit stores or implicit loads – through register sets, cache memories and main memory, is simulated using a fairly detailed cache model; computation time is determined using instruction timing formulae for basic arithmetic and logic operations (but note that multiple functional units are not taken into account, so timing overestimates will result for multiple-issue CPUs); and the time required for library calls needs to be supplied from empirical benchmark data. The PERFORM simulator was shown to achieve good accuracy for a Jacobi iteration example, but took about the same amount of time to run as the actual program [121]. In the same paper, Hey and Dunlop also presented results that showed that cache behaviour could also have a direct effect on message-passing performance. Using a tool based on Lebep [83], they showed that the message-passing time for strided data (for example, communication of a row of a matrix stored by column) could be significantly different than for contiguous data. Using PVM on a Meiko CS2 they showed that the extent of memory stride could alter communication performance by up to 1000%. On a workstation cluster using MPI, however, an overhead of only 20% was observed.

By considering message-passing calls as library calls, PERFORM could also be made to simulate message-passing parallel programs. This idea was investigated by Reeve [193], although he chose to abstract over the details of serial computation. Instead, he focussed on the communication operations in a message-passing program, statically generating instruction streams for each processor based only on the total number of processors and each individual processor's identity tag. In particular, he conceived a model with six basic operations: send, receive, asynchronous send, asynchronous receive (all parameterised by message size), wait (for asynchronous operations to complete) and work (parameterised by a number of floating point operations). Although very thin on details, Reeve explained that the instruction streams could be deterministically evaluated using two queues for each process, to represent local execution time and potential communication events [193]. Whenever two processes participating in a communication become ready, their local execution time could simply be incremented according to a model of communication time; Reeve chose to use a linear latency/bandwidth model with bandwidth sharing, ignoring non-linear network contention. The results and discussion presented by Reeve suggest that this is reasonable for a small number of processors, but that detailed contention effects for the interconnect network and memory hierarchy will play a significant role when run on a larger machine. While the work described above has made good progress at accounting for the memory hierarchy, a related study by Hernandez and Hey [120] claims that substantial effort is still needed to marry the performance results of low-level communication benchmarks with the performance achieved in real parallel codes.

Chapter 23

Becker *et al.*

In 1997, Becker and his colleagues from the Whitney project published a paper [21] that developed several simple models of NASA's NAS Parallel Benchmarks (NPB) version 2 [17]. The models were used to explore the performance trade-offs involved in building a balanced parallel cluster computer capable of supporting scientific workloads. The models that were developed were simple analytical expressions using the number and size of messages sent by each benchmark. Coupled with measurements of single processor performance, network latency and network bandwidth, these models were used to predict performance and hence find a well balanced machine for running NPB-type applications.

It was recognised that the parameter space for cluster design was quite large. Designers must consider factors such as CPU type, the amount and type of memory per node, the network technology and topology, and operating operating system. The Whitney team's design goal was to choose the most suitable configuration of a machine for a certain code based on metrics of speed, efficiency and financial cost. Clearly, not every possible cluster architecture could be physically tried. Thus, by developing simple abstract models of the NPB benchmarks as representatives of the target workload, the Whitney project evaluated the effectiveness of various architectures by calculation and simulation.

The architectural model they used for the system was characterised by network latency l in seconds, bandwidth b in bytes per second, single node performance f in operations per second, the number of nodes p and monetary hardware cost. This allowed the comparison of different technologies, for example Fast Ethernet versus Myrinet, at any given price. The communication model they used for calculating the message-passing time was $msgtime = l + message\ size/b$. The program models for each of the NPB benchmarks were created by hand and were parameterised by the number of iterations i, the total number of operations required to complete the benchmark m, and the grid size used by the benchmark. The overall time for a benchmark could then be calculated by:

$$time = m/f + i * comm(n, p, b, l)$$

where $comm(n, p, b, l)$ represented the total communication time of the code. For example, the completion time for the "BT class A" benchmark was modelled by an equation representing the three communication phases of the algorithm:

$$6 * msgtime * (\sqrt{p} - 1) * \frac{n^2}{p} * 2 * 5 * 8$$
$$+ 3 * msgtime * (\sqrt{p} - 1) * \frac{n^2}{p} * 2 * (25 + 5) * 8$$
$$+ 3 * msgtime * (\sqrt{p} - 1) * \frac{n^2}{p} * 2 * 5 * 8$$

A verification of this model using four nodes and Fast Ethernet was presented. The model predicted overall run-time to within 30%. However, the analysis of the situation was questionable because the modelled situation was dominated by computation, which is relatively easy to model accurately, while the communication cost, which is more difficult to model, was severely underestimated. Importantly, the analysis process would tend to underestimate the communication cost even more if the number of nodes were increased.

Chapter 24

Gautama

The low-cost performance analysis techniques developed for PAMELA by van Gemund (see Section 20) had assumed that model parameters were deterministic. This assumption ignored the fact that data-dependencies could significantly alter program execution. Schopf and Berman [212] had shown that the use of stochastic values for model parameters could give far more insightful predictions of parallel program execution time than single point values. In 1998, Gautama [91] added statistical distributions to the PAMELA performance modelling approach, although it was primarily focused on PAMELA's serial constructs rather than its parallel constructs, which were too difficult to analyse. Gautama characterised the probability distribution function (PDF) of model parameters using statistical moments including mean, variance, skewness and kurtosis. His treatment was mainly mathematical and did not focus on the sources of variability for the distributions. Instead, his raw data were obtained from trace-driven simulation over many runs of manually instrumented source code. While Gautama's work was not focused on parallel performance modelling, the notion of generating performance distributions is particularly relevant to the performance prediction of parallel programs, because parallel programs tend to exhibit variable performance even more than regular serial programs.

Chapter 25

Tam and Wang

An important part of modelling parallel programs is understanding the communication network that they use [156, 196, 224, 232, 234]. Tam's PhD thesis published in 2001 [237] and a related publication with Wang in 1999 [238] recognised that modern parallel architectures were converging towards machines built around collections of general purpose nodes with local memory, interfaced to each other through a reliable and scalable network. Taking this into account, they developed a performance model for communication in such networks. In their model, costs were induced by data movement through an extended memory hierarchy, consisting of a node's local cache and memory, and remote memory based at other nodes. A detailed investigation was made of the common physical and operating system processes that supported this data movement. The data movement from a sender's memory to a receiver's memory was abstracted by three phases. In the first of these, send time O_s was characterised by the expression $O_s(m) = \kappa_s + \tau_s m$ where κ_s accounted for any initial operating system queueing overhead and $\tau_s m$ accounted for the time associated with buffer copying a message of size m. In the second phase, transfer time L through the network was modelled using the costs associated with connection setup and finite bandwidth. Contention in the network was modelled by introducing a send gap g_s between output packets from a node, as well as a minimum service time at network routers g_r. In the final phase, asynchronous receives were characterised using O_r, which was analogous to O_s for the send time, plus U_r which represented the time for the receiving process at user level to access the new data using a polling scheme, or to un-block and wake-up. To test their modelling system, models of a gather operation [238] and complete exchange operation [237] were constructed. In contrast to existing models of point-to-point message-passing performance, Tam and Wang's detailed studies showed that the overall execution times for these collective operations are dominated by network contention and congestive packet loss, the effects of which are very difficult to quantify.

Chapter 26

Kranzlmüller and Schaubschläger

The only substantial attempts to tackle head-on the problem of simulating non-determinism in message-passing programs seem to have been performed by Kranzlmüller in 1992 [142] and (extended by) Schaubschläger in 2000 [208]. In general, the dynamic computation and communication structure of message-passing programs can evolve non-deterministically, depending on the exact times when messages are sent; these times vary because of processor speed, process scheduling, processor load, cache effects, memory contention, network contention, interactions with inherently non-deterministic physical processes, randomly generated input data (which is common in scientific simulation), or even dynamic program structure itself. This last situation introduces a feedback loop, where non-determinism begets yet more non-determinism. In such cases, non-determinism will obviously play a critical role in program execution. A very common parallelisation technique that exhibits this behaviour is the simple master-slave task farm, where the master distributes small work parcels to slave processes as they become idle.

The most difficult aspect of modelling non-determinism is that it introduces a potentially exponential number of different possible execution paths for any given input data. This greatly amplifies the risk of many problems, such as deadlock, livelock and race conditions. Kranzlmüller and Schaubschläger's work was aimed at automatically testing message-passing parallel programs for these problems to aid in the debugging purposes. In particular, they created a NOn-deterministic Program Evaluator (NOPE) that could record and replay program execution up to points where non-deterministic choice could occur, systematically make every possible choice, and thereby recurse through all possible program execution sequences. These executions could then be automatically validated for the absence of livelock, deadlocks and race conditions. While this work was not directly related to performance modelling, many of their ideas are extremely relevant here.

In order to determine a program's computation and communication structure, Kranzlmüller created an instrumented MPI library that could log the entry and exit points of all communication routines. Special consideration was given to the crucial points at which non-determinism could occur. These fundamental points are encountered during wildcard receives. In contrast to an explicit receive operation where the destination process is listening for a message from a specific process, in a wildcard receive the destination process does not care about the source of incoming messages – it will simply accept the first message to arrive from any source. Therefore, all wildcard receive operations imply a point of non-deterministic choice. In order to evaluate every different choice that could possibly occur in these situations, NOPE checkpoints program execution and, using Lamport's "happened-before" concept of causal dependence [145], systematically selects any possible inbound message to pair with the wildcard receive. This choice will be recorded and the program will be allowed to continue; depth-first traversal will eventually yield all possible execution paths.

Unfortunately, it is completely intractable to actually evaluate all possible program execution sequences, even for relatively short running parallel programs. Therefore, it is necessary to try and identify event orderings that are likely to happen and thus prune the tree of possible execution sequences to test. Schaubschläger recorded the event orderings of several highly non-deterministic benchmark programs on two parallel machines. He discovered that despite the huge number of event sequences that could theoretically occur, only a small number of event orderings were ever observed in practice. For example, for one application run on an nCUBE-2 with 7 points of non-determinism, hence $7! = 5040$ possible execution paths, only 116 of those paths occurred in 10 million runs. In fact, 96% of the executions resulted in one of only 3 different execution paths. On a heavily loaded Origin2000 running the same application, 100 paths accounted for 80% of 10 million runs; for the same machine in an unloaded state, 100 paths accounted for 92% of 10 million runs. Schaubschläger's basic conclusion was that network topology and load means that some messages are more likely to be preferentially received, for example because of the number of hops required to get from source to destination. Thus, if the communication time for particular messages could be accurately estimated, that information could be used to steer NOPE to only evaluate the most probable executions.

To achieve this, Schaubschläger used a modified version of a tool called SKaMPI [197, 198] to try and accurately benchmark the communication performance of the nCUBE-2 and Origin2000. By making measurements using both lightly and heavily loaded networks he discovered that contention can cause extreme variation in communication times. At this point he became discouraged and proclaimed that:

> "making exact predictions about message transfer times on a heavily loaded [parallel machine] seems impossible ... this makes predictions hardly possible and our desired estimations too inaccurate." [208]

In acquiescence to this setback, fixed latency/bandwidth parameters were chosen to model message-passing time in NOPE, although Schaubschläger lamented the inadequacies of that approach.

Finally, it is important to make two points about the direct applicability of this work to performance modelling. Firstly, it requires message-passing programs to be actually executed for each possible event ordering that is chosen for simulation; this is immensely slow. Secondly, the presented algorithms do not handle timestamps accurately during artificial replay; only information about the ordering of events is preserved. Hence, as it is, the system cannot be used for performance modelling.

Chapter 27

Magnusson *et al.*; Hughes *et al.*

Several tools are able to directly simulate program execution at the instruction set level of an architecture, and hence determine performance. Simics [152, 248], for example, is able to precisely simulate complete computer systems including the operating system and its device drivers as well as user programs on a huge variety of hardware platforms. Simics is an instruction level simulator that is able to accurately model complex cache and memory behaviour and out-of-order processing, although it does have some limitations. Other advantages of the simulation approach are that debugging sessions and performance analyses are completely non-intrusive, can access arbitrarily detailed information and can be started, stopped or replayed at will. In addition, because Simics exactly simulates entire computer systems, it is able to simulate complete communication stacks, and hence multiprocessor parallel computers. It is, however, up to the user to specify timing models for network transfers, although a default model exists. The default model for network communication uses fixed latency and bandwidth parameters. While this allows deterministic simulation, it is unrealistic because it does not account for contention. Since parallel programs are typically heavily dependent on communication performance, more accurate network models are obviously a necessity for accurate simulation results.

Rsim is another widely used instruction-level simulation tool [128, 202]. Unlike Simics, Rsim does not support full system simulation. It only simulates statically linked Sparc v9 binaries and ignores the operating system entirely. In its favour, however, Rsim is able to accurately simulate Instruction Level Parallelism (ILP), multithreading and CC-NUMA architectures. The default network model used by Rsim is a wormhole routed 2D mesh network, complete with contention and buffer space modelling. Like Simics, it is also possible to replace the network model with more accurate network simulators. For example, the SICOSYS communication simulator, which is capable of determining parallel application performance using arbitrary communication topologies and common traffic patterns, has been integrated in Rsim (see [188, 189]).

While tools like Simics and Rsim are extremely accurate, they have one major drawback: they are extremely slow. For example, Simics is only able to simulate applications at about 1/80 to 1/350 of their native speed, depending on architecture. Because Rsim also simulates ILP it is even slower and can only simulate applications at about 1/2400 to 1/7100 of their native speed. Obviously these tools run counter to one of the requirements of a performance prediction system for designing parallel algorithms: it needs to be fast. Performance predictions using these tools would take many, many times longer than actually implementing different algorithms and measuring their performance. These methods are still useful, however, for accurately simulating application performance on hypothetical or difficult to obtain parallel machines, albeit slowly. The main reason for the existence of these tools is to help hardware, operating system and compiler designers optimise the performance of very low level operations – it is not for simulating full scientific workloads.

Chapter 28

Grove and Coddington

Grove's 2003 PhD dissertation [103] presented a new, unified technique for modelling the performance of parallel programs, based on a Performance Evaluating Virtual Parallel Machine (PEVPM) [103, 109]. It was designed to overcome the lack of easy to use yet sufficiently accurate performance prediction methods for parallel programs, which has historically resulted in time-consuming measure-modify design approaches.

The scarcity of useful performance modelling methods is quite simply due to the notoriously complex behaviour of parallel programs, which makes it very difficult to devise adequate modelling methods. Grove argued that the main contributor to this complexity is contention, which causes non-deterministic delays and therefore non-deterministic program execution – a problem that was independently recognised by Kranzlmüller and Schulz at about the same time [213]. In contrast to previous performance modelling approaches, the PEVPM system has sufficient power to accurately deal with these issues, thereby providing an opportunity to move much of the performance optimisation part of writing a parallel program to the initial design phase of the software development process, with the attendant advantages that that affords.

The PEVPM uses a novel bottom-up approach that allows the performance of message-passing codes to be modelled in a very general way. It provides a rigorous system for completely describing the salient performance features of a message-passing program written in a structural programming language (of which the combination of C and MPI was chosen as a representative example). It involves annotating existing source code or writing pseudo-code using a performance directive language to define the computation and communication structure of a parallel program. An abstract Performance Evaluating Virtual Parallel Machine then executes these performance directives to simulate the time-structure of the program, and thereby predict its performance.

Two properties make this essentially execution-driven simulation novel: 1) its ability to abstractly simulate the direct performance effects of contention; and 2) its ability to simulate the indirect performance effects caused by non-deterministic program execution due to that contention. This is achieved by dynamically creating submodels of individual computation and communication events on-the-fly using Monte Carlo sampling techniques based on data-dependencies, current contention levels in the system, and detailed probability distributions of the performance of all low-level operations for a given parallel machine. These probability distributions can either be hypothetical, or empirically determined by benchmarking. This allows the PEVPM methodology to produce highly accurate performance estimations for only a low-moderate evaluation cost.

Because a PEVPM simulation evolves in virtual time, it automatically accounts for the effects of overlapping communication with computation, load imbalance and insufficient parallelism. Coupled with its ability to explicitly model communication losses, synchronisation losses and the associated resource contention issues of each of these, the PEVPM methodology accounts for all the sources of both performance and performance loss in message-passing parallel programs. Furthermore, because all of these events can be annotated, the PEVPM is capable of automatically determining and highlighting the location and extent of performance loss due to any source; it can also automatically discover program deadlock, and help programmers trace down race conditions. This information is of crucial importance in the design of well optimised parallel programs; while it is easy to see how an application programmer could use this information, the PEVPM process and the information it can provide could potentially be integrated into tools for automatic or semi-automatic program parallelisation. Also, although the concept was only discussed but not investigated in Grove's thesis, the PEVPM could possibly be enhanced to produce entirely symbolic performance models rather than empirical ones, which would allow for even lower evaluation cost that would make the PEVPM approach even more attractive for very wide-ranging parametric-based performance optimisation.

To obtain empirical data for the performance of low-level communication operations in order to validate the PEVPM system (as described in [103, 106, 108]) Grove also constructed a new tool for benchmarking low-level MPI operations called MPIBench [103, 104]. In addition to providing the standard functionality available in existing benchmarks, namely the ability to test the performance of many operations using different message sizes and in some cases using different communication patterns, MPIBench provides extra functionality to overcome some important inadequacies of these existing techniques. Firstly, MPIBench is topology-aware, and is specifically designed to ensure meaningful results on clusters of SMP nodes. Secondly, MPIBench uses an accurate global clock to measure the performance characteristics of all of the processes in an MPI program rather than simply measuring the time required for round-trip messages or collective operations at a single process. This is especially important for measuring the complex performance characteristics of collective operations. Thirdly, and crucially, the extremely fine resolution of the global clock in MPIBench allows timing data on individual MPI operations to be obtained, rather than the average time over a large number of repetitions of an MPI operation. This gives MPIBench the unique ability to accurately quantify the performance variability of MPI operations due to contention, which it does by producing probability distributions of the performance of everything that it measures. MPIBench has been used extensively for this purpose [105, 113–115, 246].

For his dissertation, Grove used MPIBench to benchmark the MPI communication performance of three large parallel computers. An extensive performance analysis of both point-to-point and collective communication was undertaken. For point-to-point operations, it was demonstrated that performance variability due to contention can be very significant; these effects are especially prevalent when large numbers of processes on distinct nodes are communicating concurrently and/or when processes in the same SMP are communicating concurrently, and even more so when transmitting large messages and/or using bidirectional communication. Furthermore, an analysis of the probability distributions describing point-to-point message-passing performance in the presence of contention showed that the Pearson 5 distribution can best explain the results observed [107]. In the future, it would be valuable to extend MPIBench so that it can automatically fit measured data from point-to-point tests to Pearson 5 distributions and plot the resultant fit parameters across a range of message sizes and contention levels. While plots of the Pearson 5 location parameter will closely resemble existing (minimum) latency graphs, the accompanying shape and scale parameters will present important yet easily digestible information about performance in the face of contention. In his thesis, Grove also presented a study of systematic outliers that were observed in performance measurements. In particular, the causes of these very slow message-passing times were identified – mainly operating system interruptions and retransmission of lost messages – and the adverse performance effects that they impose on parallel programs were discussed.

MPIBench was also used to accurately characterise the performance of collective communication on the same three parallel machines for which point-to-point communication was examined. In particular, these experiments were analysed in detail to determine either the means by which *MPI_Bcast*, *MPI_Barrier*, *MPI_Scatter*, *MPI_Gather*, *MPI_Alltoall* and their variants were constructed from constituent point-to-point messages, or whether those operations were hardware-assisted. In the case of collective operations constructed from point-to-point operations, performance models of those operations were built from the bottom-up using performance models for their constituent point-to-point operations. Each performance model of a collective operation was used to analyse the performance of the algorithm, and was also used as a small validation of the PEVPM modelling approach. In the case of hardware-assisted collective operations, the benchmark results were obtained to serve as stand-alone empirical performance models.

It is also worth summarising the major results of these group communications analyses, which were interesting in their own right. It was graphically demonstrated that there can be vast differences in the time that individual processes take to complete their part in collective operations, attested to by the wide and complicated performance profiles that were observed; for example Pascal's Triangle-shaped probability distribution functions (PDFs) were observed for software-based *MPI_Bcast*s and saw-tooth-shaped PDFs were observed for *MPI_Scatter*s. While such behaviour has been alluded to in other studies, none have made a significant attempt to quantify it. Grove's thesis, however, provided in-depth analyses, and in particular demonstrated that the standard MPI performance benchmarking technique of measuring average completion time for collective operations at one process is completely inadequate. Once a thorough understanding of the general shape of the performance profile for an operation is gained, however, average completion times can provide valuable summary information for the wary. Sometimes, however, these performance profiles can be very complicated, and even chaotic. This was demonstrated for the *MPI_Alltoall* operation on a commodity Beowulf cluster; in this case, the PDF-approach to MPI performance benchmarking made it possible to explain that the very poor performance that was observed was due to massive contention causing packet loss and subsequent network timeouts. Uncovering the source of this deficiency would have been very difficult, if in fact it was not completely overlooked using performance benchmarking tools other than MPIBench.

Grove's thesis [103] and related work [106, 108] concluded with compelling evidence in support of the usefulness of the PEVPM approach to the prediction of parallel program performance. Unlike previous performance prediction techniques, the PEVPM approach was shown to be completely general, arbitrarily flexible, very cost-effective and extremely accurate.

The generality of the PEVPM modelling system was demonstrated by its applicability to programs drawn from each of the three possible classes of parallel code – those with regular-local communication (via an example Jacobi Iteration), those with irregular communication (via a Bag of Tasks code) and those with regular-global communication (via a two-dimensional Fast Fourier Transform) – all of which were executed on a wide range of parallel machines from low-end cluster computers, though middle-of-the-range off-the-shelf supercomputers, to high-end national supercomputing hardware. The use of symbolic quantities in PEVPM directives (demonstrated for the Jacobi Iteration example) highlighted the flexibility of the PEVPM approach. Once the complete PEVPM model of a code is built up from fundamental computation and communication instructions, it can be easily evaluated and re-evaluated for different input data or machine characteristics. This gives the PEVPM the ability to support parametric performance studies, for instance to determine the best (i.e. fastest, or most efficient, or most economical, etc) parallel machine with which to solve a given code.

The PEVPM modelling technique is also very cost-effective. In addition to allowing parametric performance studies of any particular code, the low cost of model creation makes it possible to build and simulate the performance of many alternative algorithmic solutions to any given problem. As shown for the Jacobi Iteration code, PEVPM models are easy to create (for either real or hypothetical codes) through simply applying the rules for PEVPM directives. One recent modelling system called Performance Prophet [185], which is quite similar to PEVPM although it relies on relatively simplistic network modelling and hence suffers substantial inaccuracy for even medium sized machines, allows users to construct performance models using a graphical UML editor. Importantly, however, these manual modelling steps could be carried out by an automated compiler with little or no human intervention. While an automated compiler was not actually developed for Grove's thesis, creating such a compiler would be a useful future endeavour – and one recent modelling system called PEMPI [163] has made some progress along these lines, although like Performance Prophet above it relies on relatively simplistic network modelling and hence suffers the same inaccuracies. The second facet of the PEVPM's cost-effectiveness is the relative cheapness with which PEVPM models can be solved. The PEVPM simulation of the Jacobi Iteration code, for example, was carried out at 67.5 times the speed of the code's actual execution. While the speedup that will be achieved using any given PEVPM simulation will depend heavily on model granularity, most PEVPM models should be quite inexpensive to evaluate.

Finally, Grove's publications clearly demonstrated the superior accuracy of PEVPM predictions compared to the predictions made by previous performance estimation techniques. In particular, all of the case studies presented in those publications highlight how inaccurate performance predictions will be if contention effects are ignored – and recent work by Evans and Hood *et al.* [75, 76] provides corroborating evidence for these conclusions. Grove showed that contention effects were especially clear in the performance predictions for parallel codes running on clusters of SMP nodes, where contention was seen to be far more extensive. It was also shown that overall parallel application performance suffers horribly in the face of extensive communication protocol timeouts (such as were observed during an *MPI_Alltoall* operation on a typical Beowulf cluster). Unlike the PEVPM, which explicitly accounts for these outlying events, no previous performance modelling systems take such communication delays into account.

Chapter 29

SciDAC PERC and PERI

The value of performance modelling and prediction for parallel programs is certainly becoming more and more clear. In late 2001, for example, the Performance Evaluation Research Center (PERC) was established under the US Government Department of Energy's Scientific Discovery through Advanced Computing (SciDAC) program. The main aims of this activity were to understand the key factors in application codes and computer systems that affect performance, to develop benchmarks to aid in performance analyses, and to develop models for accurately predicting the performance of real world applications, in particular for codes of interest to the Department of Energy. Led by David Bailey at Lawrence Berkeley National Laboratory and Jack Dongarra at the University of Tennessee, the PERC program published about fifty papers on performance modelling for supercomputing applications between 2001 and 2005. When the PERC program finished in 2005 it was replaced by the SciDAC Performance Engineering Research Institute (PERI), which had published another twenty or so performance related papers by the middle of 2007.

One significant contribution to this substantial body of work includes that by Laura Carrington, Allan Snavely and Nicole Wolter *et al.*, who through a series of papers [40–43, 225, 226] developed a simple yet effective method of predicting the performance of scientific applications on current and future HPC platforms. Their approach requires a three step process: (1) developing an application signature using the MetaSim Tracer for collecting memory traces and MPIDtrace to collect MPI event logs; (2) developing a machine profile for low-level operations including memory loads and stores, floating point operations and communications performance; and (3) "convolving", or combining these models, using MetaSim Convolver for models of serial code and Dimemas for modelling communication events. Although these convolved models could be considered to be relatively inaccurate – typically having errors of 20% or more – compared to some of the other approaches explored earlier in this chapter, these results were obtained for very little modelling effort. It is possible, however, that even these relatively inaccurate expectations may be overly optimistic if applied in lots of other cases, as the applications studied were compute rather than communication bound; as shown in Section 28, codes with heavy communication load scale much worse than predicted by the simple linear latency/bandwidth communication models that were used here.

Despite the relative inaccuracy of these models, however, this was outweighed by the value of being able to obtain the models so cheaply. Because the models were so affordable in terms of both generation and solution time, they were actually able to be applied to a number of real-world codes on real-world supercomputing platforms. The real lesson to learn from this then, seems to be that perhaps when it comes to performance modelling the perfect really *is* the enemy of the good – at least for now. Despite this, it is quite reasonable to expect that many of the tools made available through the well resourced PERC and PERI programs will eventually be refined to include more accurate models of low-level operations – in particular those for network operations – and accuracy could be greatly improved.

Chapter 30
Conclusion

The specific performance modelling techniques for parallel programs that have been presented in this chapter are by no means exhaustive. An enormous number of other general performance modelling techniques as well as models of specific systems have been proposed, such as those by Blasko [25–30], Fleischmann [86, 87], Foster [44], Halderen [112], Juurlink *et al.* [132, 134], Kerbyson and Nudd and Papaefstathiou *et al.* [138, 173, 174, 176–178], Mohan [166], Moritz and Frank and Al-Tawil [5, 167], Nelson [170], Nicol [171], Norman and Thanisch [172], Prakash [186, 187], Riley [200], Shaw [215], Sötz [229], Wabnig and Haring [250], Wen and Fox [252], Worlton [255] and more [16, 36, 138, 143, 147, 184, 235, 254]. Many further techniques have been proposed [13, 14, 82, 84, 85, 211, 212, 256] to take into account specific problems for the increasingly abundant class of cluster computers [11, 65, 123, 199, 233, 251]. Recently, performance models have also begun appearing for programs running on the Grid [89], such as that of Bu and Xu [110].

The techniques that were presented in this chapter are, however, sufficient to introduce the difficulties that are involved with modelling the performance of parallel programs on a wide range of parallel architectures. It is these difficulties that the majority of the research community have reached consensus on; the plethora of different solutions that have been proposed merely serve to indicate that the answers to these difficulties remain to be comprehensively resolved. Perhaps, eventually, the parallel computing community will perfect and productise a simple-to-use modelling technique that is able to accurately and cost-effectively model arbitrary parallel programs on arbitrary parallel computers – and thus improve supercomputing acquisition decisions and also provide programmers with insightful details that will help them improve the performance of their programs.

References

[1] V.S. Adve. *Analyzing the Behavior and Performance of Parallel Programs*. PhD thesis, University of Wisconsin, Computer Sciences Department, December 1993.

[2] V.S. Adve and M.K. Vernon. The influence of random delays on parallel execution times. In *Proceedings of the ACM SIGMETRICS Conference on Measurement and Modeling of Computer Systems*, pages 61–73, May 1993.

[3] T. Agerwala. An analysis of controlling agents for asynchronous processes. Technical Report 35, Johns Hopkins Computer Science Program, August 1974.

[4] Alok Aggarwal, Ashok K. Chandra, and Marc Snir. On communication latency in PRAM computations. In *Proceedings of the DAGS/PC Symposium*, pages 76–86, 1993.

[5] Khalid Al-Tawil and Csaba Andras Moritz. Performance modeling and evaluation of MPI. *Journal of Parallel and Distributed Computing*, **61**(2):202–223, 2001.

[6] R. Alur, C. Courcoubetis, and D. Dill. Model-checking for probabilistic real-time systems. In *Proceedings of the 18th International Conference on Automata, Languages and Programming (LNCS 510)*, 1991.

[7] R. Alur and D.L. Dill. A theory of timed automata. *Theoretical Computer Science*, **126**:183–236, April 1994.

References

[8] G.M. Amdahl. Validity of the single-processor approach to achieving large scale computing capabilities. *Proceedings of the American Federation of Information Processing Societies*, **30**:483–485, 1967.

[9] Yair Amir, Baruch Awerbuch, Amnon Barak, Ryan S. Borgstrom, and Arie Keren. An opportunity cost approach for job assignment and reassignment in a scalable computing cluster. In *Proceedings of the 10th IASTED International Conference on Parallel and Distributed Computing Systems*, 1998.

[10] H.H. Ammar, S.M.R. Islam, M. Ammar, and S. Deng. Performance modeling of parallel algorithms. In *Proceedings of the International Conference on Parallel Processing*, volume **3**, pages 68–71, 1990.

[11] T.E. Anderson, D.E. Culler, D.A. Patterson, and The NOW team. A case for NOW (Networks Of Workstations). *IEEE Micro*, pages 54–64, February 1995.

[12] Cosimo Anglano. Predicting parallel applications performance on nondedicated cluster platforms. In *Proceedings of Supercomputing*, pages 172–179, 1998.

[13] Remzi H. Arpaci, Andrea C. Dusseau, Amin M. Vahdat, Lok T. Liu, Thomas E. Anderson, and David A. Patterson. The interaction of parallel and sequential workloads on a network of workstations. In *Proceedings of the ACM SIGMETRICS Conference on Measurement and Modeling of Computer Systems*, 1995.

[14] Remzi H. Arpaci, Amin M. Vahdat, Tom Anderson, and Dave Patterson. Combining parallel and sequential workloads on a NOW. Technical Report CSD-94-838, University of California Berkeley, Computer Science Department, 1994.

[15] D. Atapattu and D. Gannon. Building analytical models into an interactive prediction tool. In *Proceedings of Supercomputing*, pages 521–530, 1989.

[16] Rajive Bagrodia, Ewa Deelman, Steven Docy, and Thomas Phan. Performance prediction of large parallel applications using parallel simulations. In *Proceedings of the ACM SIGPLAN Symposium on the Principles and Practice of Parallel Programming*, May 1999.

[17] D. Bailey, E. Barszcz, J. Barton, D. Browning, et al. The NAS parallel benchmarks. *International Journal of Supercomputer Applications*, **5**(3):63–73, 1991.

[18] Mark Baker and Geoffrey Fox. MPI on NT: The current status and performance of the available environments. In *Proceedings of the 5th European PVM/MPI Users' Group Meeting (LNCS 1497)*, pages 63–75, September 1998.

[19] V. Balasundaram, G. Fox, K Kennedy, and U. Kremer. A static performance estimator to guide data partitioning decisions. In *Proceedings of the 3rd ACM SIGPLAN Symposium on PPoPP*, April 1991.

[20] Deb Banerjee, Thomas Tysinger, and Wayne Smith. A scalable high-performance environment for fluid flow analysis on unstructured grids. In *Proceedings of Supercomputing*, pages 8–17, 1994.

[21] Jeffrey C. Becker, Bill Nitzberg, and Rob F. Van der Wijngaart. Predicting cost/performance trade-offs for Whitney: A commodity computing cluster. In *Proceedings of the 31st Hawaii International Conference on System Sciences*, volume 7, pages 504–513, January 1998.

[22] B. Beizer. *Micro Analysis of Computer System Performance*. Van Nostrand Reinhold, New York, 1978.

[23] G Bilardi, K.T. Herley, A. Pietracaprina, G. Pucci, and P. Spirakis. BSP vs LogP. In *Proceedings of the 8th Annual ACM Symposium on Parallel Algorithms and Architectures*, pages 25–32, June 1996.

[24] L.S. Blackford, A. Cleary, J. Choi, Dongarra, et al. LAPACK working note 93 installation guide for ScaLAPACK, May 1997.

[25] R. Blasko. Automatic modeling and performance analysis of parallel processes by PEPSY. In *Proceedings of the ASIM Symposium*, pages 241–246, October 1994.

[26] R. Blasko. Process graph and tool for performance analysis of parallel processes. In *Proceedings of the IMACS Symposium on Mathematical Modeling*, pages 60–64, February 1994.

[27] R. Blasko. A systematic strategy for performance prediction by improvement of parallel programs. In *Proceedings of the 4th International Workshop on Computer Aided Systems Technology*, May 1994.

[28] R. Blasko. Hierarchical performance prediction for parallel programs. In *Proceedings of the IEEE International Symposium on Systems Engineering of Computer Based Systems*, pages 398–405, March 1995.

[29] R. Blasko. Simulation based performance prediction by PEPSY. In *Proceedings of the 28th Annual IEEE Simulation Symposium*, pages 341–349, April 1995.

[30] R. Blasko. Performance analysis of parallel programs based on simulation. In *Proceedings of the 20th ASU Conference*, pages 70–79, September 1999.

[31] S.H. Bokhari. A shortest tree algorithm for optimal assignments across space and time in a distributed processor system. *IEEE Transactions on Software Engineering*, **7**(6):583–589, 1981.

[32] Shahid H. Bokhari. On the mapping problem. *IEEE Transactions on Computers*, **30**(3):207–214, 1981.

[33] Shahid H. Bokhari. Partitioning problems in parallel, pipelined and distributed computing. *IEEE Transactions on Computers*, **37**(1):48–57, 1988.

[34] Thomas Brëanl. *Parallel Programming - An Introduction*, chapter 3. Prentice-Hall, Englewood Cliffs, New Jersey, 1993.

[35] T.H. Bredt and E.J. McCluskey. A model for parallel computer systems. Technical Report STAN-CS-70-160, Stanford University, Digital Systems Laboratory, April 1970.

[36] J. Brehm, L. Dowdy, M. Madhukar, and E. Smirni. PrePreT - a performance prediction tool. In *Quantitative Evaluation of Computing and Communication Systems (LNCS 977)*. Springer-Verlag, 1995.

[37] Stephen D. Brookes. On the relationship of CCS and CSP. In *Advanced NATO Study Institute on Logics and Models for Verification and Specification of Concurrent Systems*. Institut National de Recherche en Informatique et Automatique, 1984.

[38] H. Burkhart, C. Falcó Korn, S. Gutzwiller, P. Ohnacker, and S. Waser. BACS: Basel Algorithm Classification Scheme. Technical Report 93-3, Institut für Informatik der Universität Basel, March 1993.

[39] Nick Carriero, Eric Freeman, David Gelernter, and David Kaminsky. Adaptive parallelism and piranha. *IEEE Computer*, **28**(1):40–49, January 1995.

[40] L. Carrington, R. Campbell, and L. Davis. How well can simple metrics represent the performacne of HPC applications? In *Proceedings of Supercomputing*, November 2005.

[41] L. Carrington, A. Snavely, X. Gao, and N. Wolter. A performance prediction framework for scientific applications. *Future Generation Computer Systems*, **22**(3):336–346, 2006.

[42] L. Carrington, N. Wolter, and A. Snavely. A framework for application performance prediction to enable scalability understanding. In *Scaling to New Heights Workshop*, May 2002.

[43] L. Carrington, N. Wolter, A. Snavely, and C. Baily Lee. Applying and automated framework to prodce accurate blind performance predictions of full-scale HPC applications. In *Proceedings of UGC*, 2004.

[44] K.M. Chandy and I. Foster. A deterministic notation for cooperating processes. *IEEE Transactions on Parallel and Distributed Systems*, **6**(8):863–871, 1995.

[45] B.M. Chapman, P. Mehrotra, and H.P. Zima. Extending HPF for advanced data parallel applications. In *IEEE Magazine on Parallel and Distributed Technology*, pages 59–70, 1994.

References

[46] J. Choi, J.J. Dongarra, R. Pozo, and D.W. Walker. Scalapack: A scalable linear algebra library for distributed memory concurrent computers. In *Proceedings of the 4th Symposium on the Frontiers of Massively Parallel Computation*, pages 120–127, 1992.

[47] Yuan-Chieh Chow and Walter H. Kohler. Models for dynamic load balancing in a heterogeneous multiple processor system. *IEEE Transactions on Computers*, **28**(5):354–361, 1979.

[48] Mark J. Clement and Michael J. Quinn. Multivariate statistical techniques for parallel performance prediction. In *Proceedings of the 28th Hawaii International Conference on System Sciences*, volume **2**, pages 446–455, January 1995.

[49] Mark J. Clement and Michael J. Quinn. Automated performance prediction for scalable parallel computing. *Parallel Computing*, **10**(23):1405–1420, 1997.

[50] Mark J. Clement, Michael R. Steed, and Phyllis E. Crandall. Network performance modeling for PVM clusters. In *Proceedings of Supercomputing*, November 1996.

[51] M. Cole. Algorithmic skeletons: Structured management of parallel computation. In *Research Monographs in Parallel and Distributed Computing*. The MIT Press, Cambridge, Massachusetts, 1989.

[52] R. Cole and O. Zajicek. The APRAM: Incorporating asynchrony in the PRAM model. In *Proceedings of the 1989 ACM Symposium on Parallel Algorithms and Architectures*, pages 169–178, June 1989.

[53] Compaq Computer Corporation, Intel Corporation, and Microsoft Corporation. Virtual Interface Architecture specification, December 1997.

[54] Mark E. Crovella and Thomas J. LeBlanc. Parallel performance prediction using lost cycles analysis. In *Proceedings of Supercomputing*, pages 600–609, 1994.

[55] M.E. Crovella. *Performance Prediction and Tuning of Parallel Programs*. PhD thesis, University of Rochester, 1994.

[56] D. Culler, R. Karp, D. Patterson, A. Sahay, K.E. Schauser, E. Santos, R. Subruamonian, and T. Eicken. LogP: Towards a realistic model of parallel computation. In *Proceedings of the 5th ACM SIGPLAN Symposium on the Principles and Practices of Parallel Programming*, pages 1–12, May 1993.

[57] Zarka Cvetanovic. The effects of problem partitioning, allocation, and granularity on the performance of multiple-processor systems. *IEEE Transactions on Computers*, **36**(4):421–432, 1987.

[58] G. Cybenko, L. Kipp, L. Pointer, and D. Kuck. Supercomputer performance evaluation and the Perfect benchmarks. Technical Report 965, University of Illinois Center for Supercomputing R&D, March 1990.

[59] W.J. Dally and D.S. Willis. Universal mechanisms for concurrency. In *Proceedings of Parallel Architectures and Languages Europe (LNCS 365)*, pages 19–33, 1989.

[60] M. Danelutto, R. Do Meglio, S. Pelagatti, and M. Vanneschi. High level language constructs for massively parallel computing. In *Proceedings of the 6th International Symposium on Computer and Information Sciences*, pages 777–788, October 1991.

[61] Sajal K. Das, Daniel J. Harvey, and Rupak Biswas. Dynamic load balancing for adaptive meshes using symmetric broadcast networks. In *Proceedings of the 12th ACM International Conference on Supercomputing*, pages 417–424, 1998.

[62] J. Davies and S. Schneider. A brief history of timed CSP. *Theoretical Computer Science*, **138**(10):243–271, 1995.

[63] J.W.M Davies. *Specification and Proof in Real-Time Systems*. Cambridge University Press, Cambridge, 1993.

[64] Thomas Decker, Reinhard Luling, and Stefan Tschoke. A distributed load balancing algorithm for heterogeneous parallel computing systems. In *Proceedings of the International Conference on Parallel and Distributed Processing Techniques and Applications*, volume **2**, pages 933–940, 1998.

References

[65] Viktor K. Decyk, Dean E. Dauger, and Pieter R. Kokelaar. How to build an AppleSeed: A parallel Macintosh cluster for numerically intensive computing. In *Proceedings of the 6th International School for Space Simulation*, September 2001.

[66] E.W. Dijkstra. Solution of a problem in concurrent programming control. *Journal of the ACM*, **8**:569, 1965.

[67] E.W. Dijkstra. Cooperating sequential processes. *Programming Languages*, pages 43–112, 1968.

[68] Jack Dongarra, Hans Meuer, and Erich Strohmaier. Top 500 supercomputer sites. Available from http://www.top500.org/.

[69] J.J. Dongarra, J.R. Bunch, C.B. Moler, and Stewart G.W. *LINPACK User's Guide*. SIAM, 1979.

[70] M. Dubois and M. Briggs. Performance of synchronized iterative processes in multiprocessor systems. *IEEE Transactions on Software Engineering*, **8**:419–431, July 1982.

[71] Alistair Dunlop and Tony Hey. PERFORM - a fast simulator for estimating program execution time. *On-line Journal of Performance Evaluation and Modelling for Computer Systems*, November 1997. http://www.netlib.org/utk/papers/PEMCS/.

[72] A.N. Dunlop and D.J. Pritchard. Parallel performance estimator. Technical Report D5.3b, ESPRIT project, Department of Electronics and Computer Science, University of Southampton, 1995.

[73] Peter J. Dunning. The working set model of program behaviour. *Communications of the ACM*, **11**(5):323–333, May 1968.

[74] D.L. Eager, J. Zahorjan, and E.D. Lazowska. Speedup versus efficiency in parallel systems. *IEEE Transactions on Computers*, **38**:408–423, March 1989.

[75] J. Evans and C. Hood. Network performance variability in NOW clusters. In *Proceedings of the 5th IEEE/ACM conference on cluster computing and the Grid*, May 2005.

[76] J. Evans, C. Hood, and W. Gropp. Exploring the relationship between parallel application run-time variability and network performance. In *Workshop on High-Speed Local Networks, IEEE Conference on Local Computer Networks*, October 2003.

[77] T. Fahringer. *Automatic Performance Prediction of Parallel Programs on Massively Parallel Programs*. PhD thesis, University of Vienna, 1993.

[78] T. Fahringer. Automatically estimating network contention of parallel programs. In *Proceedings of the 7th International Conference on Modeling Techniques and Tools for Computer Performance Evaluation*, May 1994.

[79] T. Fahringer. *Automatic Performance Prediction of Parallel Programs*. Kluwer Academic, Boston, Massachusetts, 1996.

[80] T. Fahringer, R. Blasko, and H.P. Zima. Automatic performance prediction to support parallelization of Fortran programs for massively parallel systems. In *Proceedings of the 6th ACM International Conference on Supercomputing*, pages 347–356, 1992.

[81] T. Fahringer and H.P. Zima. A static parameter-based performance prediction tool for parallel programs. In *Proceedings of the 7th ACM International Conference on Supercomputing*, pages 207–219, July 1993.

[82] Rod Fatoohi and Sisira Weeratunga. Performance evaluation of three distributed computing environments for scientific applications. In *Proceedings of Supercomputing*, pages 400–409, 1994.

[83] C. Figueira and Hernández. Benchmarks specification and generation for performance estimation on MIMD machines. *IFIP Transactions on Computer Science and Technology*, 44:215–223, 1994.

[84] Silvia M. Figueira and Francine Berman. Modeling the effects of contention on the performance of heterogeneous applications. In *Proceedings of the 5th International Symposium on High Performance Distributed Computing*, August 1996.

[85] Silvia M. Figueira and Francine Berman. Predicting slowdown for networked workstations. In *Proceedings of the 6th International Symposium on High Performance Distributed Computing*, August 1997.

[86] G. Fleischmann. Performance evaluation of parallel program based on model calculations. *Parallel Computing*, **20**(10-11), November 1994.

[87] G. Fleischmann and M. Gente. Modeling and evaluation of parallel programs using GIANT. In *Proceedings of the 6th International Conference on Modelling Techniques and Tools for Computer Performance Evaluation*, September 1992.

[88] S. Fortune and J. Wyllie. Parallelism in random access machines. In *Proceedings of the 10th ACM Symposium on Theory of Computing*, pages 114–118, 1978.

[89] I. Foster and C. Kesselman (eds.). *The Grid: Blueprint for a New Computing Infrastructure*. Morgan Kaufmann, San Francisco, 1999.

[90] K. Gallivan, W. Jalby, A. Malony, and H. Wijshoff. Performance prediction for parallel numerical algorithms. *International Journal of High-Speed Computing*, **3**(1):31–62, 1991.

[91] Hasyim Gautama. A probabilistic approach to the analysis of program execution time. Master's thesis, Delft University of Technology, Information Technology and Systems, 1998.

[92] A. Geist, A. Beguelin, J. Dongarra, W. Jiang, R. Manchek, and V. Sunderam. PVM: Parallel Virtual Machine: A user's guide and tutorial for networked parallel computing, 1994.

[93] E. Gelenbe and Z. Liu. Performance analysis approximations for parallel processing in multiprocessor systems. In *Proceedings of the IFIP Working Conference on Parallel Processing*, pages 363–375, April 1988.

[94] E. Gelenbe, E. Montagne, R. Suros, and C.M. Woodside. Performance of block-structured parallel programs. In M. Cosnard et al., editors, *Parallel Algorithms and Architectures*, pages 127–138. North-Holland, Amsterdam, 1986.

[95] V. Georgitsis and J. Sobolewski. Performance of MPL and MPICH on the SP2 system. In *Proceedings of the MPI Developer's Conference*, June 1995.

[96] Vasilios Georgitsis. *Message Passing Performance on SP Systems*. PhD thesis, University of New Mexico, 1996.

[97] V.S. Getov, R.W. Hockney, and A.J.G. Hey. Performance analysis of distributed applications by suitability functions. In *Proceedings of Programming Models for Massively Parallel Computers*, pages 191–197, September 1993.

[98] S. Girona and J. Labarta. Sensitivity of performance prediction of message passing programs. In *Proceedings of the International Conference on Parallel and Distributed Processing Techniques and Applications*, pages 933–940, June 1999.

[99] S. Girona, J. Labarta, and Rosa M. Badia. Validation of Dimemas communication model for MPI collective operations. In *Proceedings of the 7th European PVM/MPI Users' Group Meeting*, September 2000.

[100] L.M. Goldschalger. A unified approach to models of synchronous parallel machines. *Journal of the ACM*, **24**(4):1073–1086, 1982.

[101] A.Y. Grama, Gupta. A, and V. Kumar. Isoefficiency: Measuring the scalability of parallel algorithms and architectures. *IEEE Parallel and Distributed Technology*, **1**(3):12–21, August 1993.

[102] William Gropp, Ewing Lusk, and Anthony Skjellum. *Using MPI: Portable Parallel Programming with the Message-Passing Interface*. The MIT Press, Cambridge, Massachusetts, 1994.

[103] D.A. Grove. *Performance Modelling of Message-Passing Parallel Programs*. PhD thesis, University of Adelaide, Department of Computer Science, May 2003.

[104] D.A. Grove and P.D. Coddington. Precise MPI performance measurement using MPIBench. In *Proceedings of HPC Asia*, September 2001.

[105] D.A. Grove and P.D. Coddington. Performance analysis of MPI communications on the AlphaServer SC. In *Proceedings of the Australian Partnership for Advanced Computing Conference*, September 2003.

[106] D.A. Grove and P.D. Coddington. Communication benchmarking and performance modelling of MPI programs on cluster computers. In *Proceedings of the Workshop on Performance Modeling, Evaluation, and Optimization of Parallel and Distributed Systems*, April 2004.

[107] D.A. Grove and P.D. Coddington. Analytical models of probability distributions for MPI point-to-point communication times on distributed memory parallel computers. In *Proceedings of the 6th International Conference on Algorithms and Architectures for Parallel Processing*, October 2005.

[108] D.A. Grove and P.D. Coddington. Communication benchmarking and performance modelling of MPI programs on cluster computers. *The Journal of Supercomputing*, **34**(2):201–217, 2005.

[109] D.A. Grove and P.D. Coddington. Modeling message-passing programs with a performance evaluating virtual parallel machine. *Performance Evaluation*, **60**(1-4):165–187, 2005.

[110] Bu Guanying and Xu Zhiwei. Grid system theoretical model. In *Proceedings of HPC Asia*, September 2001.

[111] M. Gupta and P. Banerjee. Compile-time estimation of communication costs of programs. In *Proceedings of the 2nd Workshop on Automatic Data Layout and Performance Prediction*, April 1995.

[112] B. van Halderen. A tool for application performance prediction. Master's thesis, University of Amsterdam, Department of Mathematics and Computer Science, September 1995.

[113] Nor Asilah Wati Abdul Hamid, Paul Coddington, and Francis Vaughan. Performance analysis of MPI communications on the SGI Altix 3700. In *Proceedings of the Australian Partnership for Advanced Computing Conference*, September 2005.

[114] Nor Asilah Wati Abdul Hamid, Paul Coddington, and Francis Vaughan. Comparison of MPI benchmark programs on an SGI Altix ccNUMA shared memory machine. In *Proceedings of the Workshop on Performance Modeling, Evaluation, and Optimization of Parallel and Distributed Systems*, April 2006.

[115] Nor Asilah Wati Abdul Hamid, Paul Coddington, and Francis Vaughan. Averages, distributions and scalability of MPI communication times for ethernet and myrinet networks. In *Proceedings of Parallel and Distributed Computing and Networks*, February 2007.

[116] Tim J. Harris. A survey of PRAM simulation techniques. *ACM Computing Surveys*, **26**(2):187–200, June 1994.

[117] M.T. Heath. Performance visualization with ParaGraph. In *Proceedings of the 2nd Workshop on Environments and Tools for Parallel Scientific Computing*, pages 221–230, 1994.

[118] J.L. Hennessey and D.A. Patterson. *Computer Architecture: A Quantitative Approach*. Morgan Kaufmann, San Francisco, 1996.

[119] H. Hermanns, Herzog U., U. Klehmet, V. Mertsiotakis, and M. Siegle. Compositional performance modelling with the TIPPtool. *Lecture Notes in Computer Science*, **1469**:51–62, 1998.

[120] E. Hernandez and A.J.G. Hey. White-box benchmarking. In *Proceedings of the 4th International Euro-Par Conference (LNCS 1470)*, pages 220–223, June 1998.

[121] Anthony J.G. Hey, Alistair N. Dunlop, and E. Hernández. Realistic parallel performance estimation. *Parallel Computing*, **23**(1-2):5–21, April 1997.

[122] T. Heywood and S. Ranka. A practical hierarchical model of parallel computation. *Journal of Parallel and Distributed Computing*, **16**(3):233–249, November 1992.

[123] Jim Hill, Michael Warren, and Patrick Goda. I'm not going to pay a lot for this supercomputer. *Linux Journal*, **45**, January 1998.

[124] Jonathan M.D. Hill, Bill McColl, Dan C. Stefanescu, Mark W. Goudreau, Kevin Lang, Satish B. Rao, Torsten Suel, Thanasis Tsantilas, and Rob H. Bisseling. BSPlib: The BSP programming library. *Parallel Computing*, **24**(14):1947–1980, 1998.

[125] C.A.R. Hoare. Communicating Sequential Processes. *Communications of the ACM*, **21**(8):666–677, 1978.

[126] C.A.R. Hoare. *Communicating Sequential Processes*. Prentice-Hall, Englewood Cliffs, New Jersey, 1985.

[127] R.W. Hockney. Performance parameters and benchmarking of supercomputers. *Parallel Computing*, **17**(10), December 1991.

[128] Christopher J. Hughes, Vijay S. Pai, Parthasarathy Ranganathan, and Sarita V. Adve. Rsim: Simulating shared-memory multiprocessors with ILP processors. *IEEE Computer*, February 2002.

[129] R.N. Ibbet, T. Heywood, M.I. Cole, R.J. Pooley, et al. Algorithms, architectures and models of computation. Technical Report ECS-CSG-22-96, University of Edinburgh, Division of Informatics, 1996.

[130] Nayeem Islam. Characterizing parallel and distributed applications. In *Distributed Objects*. IEEE Computer Society Press, 1996.

[131] H. Jonkers. *Performance Analysis of Parallel Systems: A Hybrid Approach*. PhD thesis, Delft University of Technology, Information Technology and Systems, October 1995.

[132] Ben H.H. Juurlink and Harry A.G. Wijshoff. Experiences with a model for parallel computation. In *Proceedings of the 12th ACM Symposium on the Principles of Distributed Computing*, pages 87–96, August 1993.

[133] Ben H.H. Juurlink and Harry A.G. Wijshoff. The E-BSP model: Incorporating general locality and unbalanced communication into the BSP model. In *Proceedings of the 2nd International Euro-Par Conference (LNCS 1124)*, 1996.

[134] Ben H.H. Juurlink and Harry A.G. Wijshoff. A quantitative comparison of parallel computation models. *ACM Transactions on Computer Systems*, **16**(3):271–318, August 1998.

[135] A. Kapelnikov, R.R. Muntz, and M.D. Ercegovac. A modeling methodology for the analysis of concurrent systems and computations. *Journal of Parallel and Distributed Computing*, **6**(3):568–597, June 1989.

[136] Richard Karp and Raymond Miller. Parallel program schema: A mathematical model for parallel computation. In *Proceedings of the 8th Annual Symposium on Switching Automata Theory*, pages 55–61, October 1967.

[137] Richard M. Karp and Raymond E. Miller. Properties of a model for parallel computations: Determinacy, termination, queueing. *SIAM Journal on Applied Mathematics*, **14**:1390–1411, November 1966.

[138] Darren Kerbyson, Hank Alme, Adolfy Hoisie, Fabrizio Petrini, Harvey Wasserman, and Mike Gittings. Predictive performance and scalability modeling of a large-scale application. In *Proceedings of Supercomputing*, November 2001.

[139] D.E. Knuth. *The Art of Computer Programming Vol. I: Fundamental Algorithms*. Addison-Wesley, Reading, Massachusetts, 1968.

[140] D.E. Knuth. Big Omicron and Big Omega and Big Theta. *ACM SIGACT News*, **8**(2):18–23, 1976.

[141] Charles Howard Koelbel. *Compiling Programs for Distributed Memory Machines*. PhD thesis, Purdue University, Department of Computer Science, 1990.

[142] D. Kranzlmüller and J. Volkert. NOPE: A nondeterministic program evaluator. In *Proceedings of the 4th International ACPC Conference (LNCS 1557)*, pages 490–499, February 1992.

[143] Vipin Kumar and Anshul Gupta. Analyzing scalability of parallel algorithms and architectures. *Journal of Parallel and Distributed Computing*, **22**(3):379–391, June 1991.

[144] J. Labarta, S. Girona, Pillet, Cortes abd T. V., and L. Gregoris. DiP: A parallel program development environment. In *Proceedings of the 2nd International Euro-Par Conference*, volume **II**, pages 665–674, August 1996.

[145] L. Lamport. Time, clocks, and the ordering of events in a distributed system. *Communications of the ACM*, **27**(7):558–565, 1978.

[146] B.P Lester. A system for computing the speedup of parallel programs. In *Proceedings of the International Conference on Parallel Processing*, pages 145–152, August 1986.

[147] C. Lin and L. Snyder. The Kheystone benchmark for parallel performance prediction. Technical Report 92-06-01, University of Washington, Department of Computer Science and Engineering, 1992.

[148] R. Lipton, L. Snyder, and Y. Zalcstein. A comparative study of models of parallel computation. In *Proceedings of the 15th Annual IEEE Symposium on Switching and Automata Theory*, pages 145–155, October 1974.

[149] Michael Lo and Sivarama P. Dandamudi. Performance of hierarchical load sharing in heterogeneous distributed systems. In *Proceedings of the 8th IASTED International Conference on Parallel and Distributed Computing Systems*, pages 370–377, 1996.

[150] G. Lowe. Probabilistic and prioritized models of timed CSP. *Theoretical Computer Science*, **138**:315–352, 1995.

[151] Gavin Lowe. *Probabilities and Priorities in Timed CSP*. PhD thesis, St. Hugh's College, Oxford University, 1993.

[152] Peter S. Magnusson, Magnus Christensson, Jesper Eskilson, Daniel Forsgren, Gustav Hllberg, Johan Högberg, Fredrik Larsson, Andreas Moestedt, and Bengt Werner. Simics: A full system simulation platform. *IEEE Computer*, February 2002.

[153] V.W. Mak. *Performance Prediction of Concurrent Systems*. PhD thesis, Stanford University, Computer Science Department, 1987.

[154] V.W. Mak and S.F. Lundstrom. Predicting performance of parallel computations. *IEEE Transactions on Parallel and Distributed Systems*, 1(3):257–270, July 1990.

[155] Gabriel Marin and John Mellor-Crummey. Cross-architecture performance predictions for scientific applications using parameterized models. In *Proceedings of SIGMETRICS/Performance*, June 2004.

[156] Richard P. Martin, Amin M. Vahdat, David E. Culler, and Thomas E. Anderson. Effects of communication latency, overhead, and bandwidth in a cluster architecture. In *Proceedings of the 24th International Symposium on Computer Architecture*, pages 85–97, 1997.

[157] W.F. McColl. Foundations of time-critical scalable computing. In *Proceedings of the 15th IFIP World Computer Congress*, pages 93–107, 1998.

[158] P. Mehra, M. Gower, and M. Bass. Automated modeling of message-passing systems. In *Proceedings of International Workshop on Modeling, Analysis and Simulation of Computer and Telecommunication Systems*, pages 187–192, January 1994.

[159] P. Mehra, C.H. Schulback, and J.C. Yan. A comparison of two model-based performance prediction techniques for message-passing parallel programs. In *Proceedings of the ACM SIGMETRICS Conference on Measurement and Modeling of Computer Systems*, pages 181–189, May 1994.

[160] C.L. Mendes, J-C Wang, and D.A. Reed. Automatic performance prediction and scalability analysis for data parallel programs. In *Proceedings of the 2nd Workshop on Automatic Data Layout and Performance Prediction*, April 1995.

[161] Message-Passing Interface Forum (MPIF). MPI-2: Extensions to the Message Passing Interface. Available from http://www.mpi-forum.org.

[162] Message-Passing Interface Forum (MPIF). MPI: A Message Passing Interface standard. Available from http://www.mpi-forum.org.

[163] Edson T. Midorikawa, Helio Oliveira, and Jean Marcos Laine. PEMPIs: A new methodology for modeling and prediction of MPI programs performance. *International Journal of Parallel Programming*, **33**(5):499–527, 2005.

[164] Robin Milner. A calculus of communicating systems. In *Lecture Notes in Computer Science (92)*. Springer-Verlag, New York, 1980.

[165] A.G. Mohamed, G.C. Fox, G. von Laszewski, M. Parashar, T. Haupt, K. Mills, Y.H. Lu, N.T. Lin, and N.K. Yeh. Application benchmark set for Fortran-D and High Performance Fortran. Technical Report SCCS-327, Northeast Parallel Architectures Center, Syracuse University, June 1992.

[166] J. Mohan. *Performance of Parallel Programs: Model and Analyses*. PhD thesis, Carnegie Mellon University, School of Computer Science, July 1984.

[167] Csaba Andras Moritz and Matthew I. Frank. LoGPC: Modeling network contention in message-passing programs. *ACM SIGMETRICS Performance Evaluation Review Special Issue*, **26**(1), 1998.

[168] Ronald Mraz. Reducing the variance of point-to-point transfers for parallel real-time programs. *Parallel and Distributed Technology*, **2**(4):20–31, 1994.

[169] T. Murata. Petri nets: Properties, analysis and applications. *Proceedings of the IEEE*, **77**:541–580, April 1989.

[170] R Nelson. A performance evaluation of a general parallel processing model. *ACM SIGMETRICS Performance Evaluation Review*, **18**(1):14–26, 1990.

[171] David Nicol and James Townsend. Accurate modeling of parallel scientific computations. In *Proceedings of the ACM SIGMETRICS Conference on Measurement and Modeling of Computer Systems*, pages 165–179, 1989.

[172] Michael G. Norman and Peter Thanisch. Models of machines and modules for mapping to minimise makespan in multicomputers. Technical Report 9114, University of Edinburgh, Edinburgh Parallel Computing Centre, 1996.

[173] G.R. Nudd, D.J. Kerbyson, Papaefstathiou E., S.C. Perry, J.S. Harper, and D.V. Wilcox. PACE - A toolset for the performance prediction of parallel and distributed systems. *The International Journal of High Performance Computing Applications*, **14**(3):228–251, Fall 2000.

[174] G.R. Nudd, E. Papaefstathiou, T. Papay, T.J. Atherton, C.T. Clarke, D.J. Kerbyson, A.F. Stratton, M.J. Zemerly, and R. Ziani. A layered approach to the characterisation of parallel systems for performance prediction. In *Proceedings of Performance Evaluation of Parallel Systems*, pages 26–34, November 1993.

[175] Pallas GmbH. Vampir home page. http://www.pallas.com/e/products/vampir/.

[176] Efstathios Papaefstathiou. *A Framework for Characterising Parallel Systems for Performance Evaluation*. PhD thesis, University of Warwick, Computer Sciences Department, September 1995.

[177] Efstathios Papaefstathiou and D.J. Kerbyson. Predicting communication delays of detailed application workloads. In *Proceedings of the 13th International Conference on Parallel and Distributed Computing Systems*, August 2000.

[178] Efstathios Papaefstathiou, D.J. Kerbyson, G.R. Nudd, and T.J. Atherton. An overview of the $CHIP_3S$ performance prediction toolset for parallel systems. In *Proceedings of the 8th International Conference on Parallel and Distributed Computing Systems*, pages 527–533, 1995.

[179] Manish Parashar. *Interpretive Performance Prediction for High Performance Parallel Computing*. PhD thesis, Syracuse University, Department of Electrical and Computer Engineering, July 1994.

[180] Manish Parashar and Salim Hariri. Interpretive performance prediction for parallel application development. *Journal of Parallel and Distributed Computing*, **60**:17–47, 2000.

[181] Jeff Parker and George Cybenko. Dynamic load balancing for distributed memory multiprocessors. *Journal of Parallel and Distributed Computing*, **7**(2):279–301, October 1989.

[182] J. Peterson and T. Bredt. A comparison of models of parallel computation. In *Proceedings of the IFIP Congress*, pages 466–470, August 1974.

[183] J. L. Peterson. *Petri Net Theory and the Modeling of Systems*. Prentice-Hall, Englewood Cliffs, New Jersey, 1981.

[184] H. Pfneiszl. Synthetic workload generation for parallel processing systems. Master's thesis, University of Vienna, Institute of Applied Computer Science, January 1996.

[185] S. Pllana and T. Fahringer. Performance Prophet: A performance modeling and prediction tool for parallel and distributed programs. In *Proceedings of the International Conference on Parallel Processing*, June 2005.

[186] S. Prakash. *Performance Prediction of Parallel Pgorams*. PhD thesis, University of California Los Angeles, Computer Science Department, 1996.

[187] S. Prakash and S. Bagrodia. Using parallel simulation to evaluate MPI programs. In *Proceedings of the Winter Simulation Conference*, December 1998.

[188] V. Puente, J.A. Gregorio, and R. Beivide. SICOSYS: An integrated framework for studying interconnection networks in multiprocessor systems. In *Proceedings of the 10th Euromicro Workshop on Parallel and Distributed Processing*, pages 15–22, 2002.

[189] V. Puente, J.M. Prellezo, C. Izu, J.A. Gregorio, and R. Beivide. A case study of trace-driven simulation for analyzing interconnection networks:

cc-NUMAs with ILP processors. In *Proceedings of the 8th Euromicro Workshop on Parallel and Distributed Processing*, January 2000.

[190] B. Qin, H.A. Sholl, and R.A. Ammar. Micro time cost analysis of parallel computations. *IEEE Transactions on Computers*, **40**:613–628, May 1991.

[191] Xiaohan Qin and Jean-Loup Baer. A performance evaluation of cluster architectures. *ACM SIGMETRICS Performance Evaluation Review*, **25**(1):237–247, June 1997.

[192] G.M. Reed and A.W. Roscoe. A timed model for CSP. In *Proccedings of ICALP (LNCS 226)*, pages 314–323, 1996.

[193] Jeff S. Reeve. A performance estimator for parallel programs. In *Proceedings of the International Euro-Par Conference*, pages 193–202, 1999.

[194] S.K. Reinhardt, M.D. Hill, J.R. Larus, A.R. Lebeck, J.C. Lewis, and D.A. Wood. The wisconsin wind tunnel: Virtual prototyping of parallel computers. In *Proceedings of the ACM SIGMETRICS Conference on Measurement and Modeling of Computer Systems*, pages 48–60, May 1993.

[195] M. Reiser and S.S. Lavenberg. Mean value analysis of closed multichain queueing networks. *Journal of the ACM*, **27**:313–322, April 1980.

[196] Chance Reschke, Thomas Sterling, Daniel Ridge, Daniel Saverese, Donald Becker, and Phillip Merkey. A design study of alternative network topologies for the Beowulf parallel workstation. In *Proceedings of the 5th International Symposium on High Performance Distributed Computing*, 1996.

[197] Ralf Reussner, Peter Sanders, and Jesper Larsson Träff. SKaMPI: A comprehensive benchmark for public benchmarking of MPI. *Scientific Computing*, **10**, 2001.

[198] Ralf H. Reussner, Peter Sanders, Lutz Prechelt, and Matthias Müller. SKaMPI: A detailed, accurate MPI benchmark. In *Proceedings of the*

5th European PVM/MPI Users' Group Meeting (LNCS 1497), pages 52–59, September 1998.

[199] Daniel Ridge, Donald Becker, Phillip Merkey, and Tomas Sterling. Beowulf: Harnessing the power of parallelism in a Pile-of-PCs. In *Proceedings of IEEE Aerospace*, 1997.

[200] Graham D. Riley. Techniques for improving the performance of parallel computations. Master's thesis, University of Manchester, 1996.

[201] A.W. Roscoe. *The Theory and Practice of Concurrency*. Prentice-Hall, Englewood Cliffs, New Jersey, 1997.

[202] Rsim Research Group. Rsim home page. Available from http://rsim.cs.uiuc.edu/rsim/.

[203] R. Saavedra and A. Smith. Analysis of benchmark characteristics and benchmark performance prediction. Technical Report USC-CS-92-524, University of Southern California Los Angeles, Computer Science Division, September 1992.

[204] R. Saavedra and A. Smith. Analysis of benchmark characteristics and benchmark performance prediction. *ACM Transactions on Computer Systems*, **14**(4):344–384, November 1996.

[205] S. Salza. Approximating response time distributions in closed queueing network models of computer performance. In *Proceedings of Performance*, pages 133–145, 1981.

[206] V. Sarkar. Determining average program execution times and their variance. In *Proceedings of the SIGPLAN Notices Conference on Programming Language Design and Implementation*, pages 298–312, 1989.

[207] Bryan Scattergood. *The Semantics and Implementation of Machine-Readable CSP*. PhD thesis, Trinity College, Oxford University, 1998.

[208] Christian Schaubschläger. Automatic testing of nondeterministic programs in message passing systems. Master's thesis, Johannes Kepler University Linz, Department for Computer Graphics and Parallel Processing, 2000.

[209] S. Schneider. An operational semantics for timed CSP. *Information and Computation*, **116**(2):193–213, February 1995.

[210] S. Schneider. *Concurrent and Real-time Systems: The CSP Approach*. Wiley, New York, 2000.

[211] J.M. Schopf. *Performance Prediction and Scheduling for Parallel Applications on Multi-user Clusters*. PhD thesis, University of California San Diego, Department of Computer Science, December 1998.

[212] J.M. Schopf and F. Berman. Performance prediction in production environments. In *Proceedings of the 12th IEEE International Parallel Processing Symposium and 9th Symposium on Parallel and Distributed Processing*, March 1998.

[213] Martin Schulz, Dieter Kranzlmüller, and Bronis R. de Supinski. Exploring unexpected behavior in MPI. In *Proceedings of Higher Performance Computing and Communications*, pages 843–852, 2006.

[214] H.T. Schwartz. Ultracomputers. *ACM Transactions on Programming Language Systems*, **2**(4):484–521, 1980.

[215] A.C. Shaw. Deterministic timing schema for parallel programs. In *Proceedings of the 5th IEEE International Parallel Processing Symposium*, pages 56–63, April 1991.

[216] Niranjan G. Shivaratri, Phillip Krueger, and Mukesh Singhal. Load distributing for locally distributed systems. *IEEE Computer*, **25**(12):33–44, 1992.

[217] Jaswinder Pal Singh, Edward Rothberg, and Anoop Gupta. Modeling communication in parallel algorithms: A fruitful interaction between theory and systems? In *Proceedings of the 6th Annual ACM Symposium on Parallel Algorithms and Architectures*, pages 189–199, 1993.

[218] David Skillicorn. *Foundations of Parallel Programming*, chapter 8, pages 123–169. Cambridge University Press, Cambridge, 1994.

[219] D.B. Skillicorn. Parallelism and the Bird-Meertens Formalism. Technical report, Queen's University, Computing and Information Science, April 1992.

[220] D.B. Skillicorn. Questions and answers about categorical data types. Technical report, Queen's University, Computing and Information Science, May 1994.

[221] D.B. Skillicorn. Abstract machine models for parallel and distributed computing. In M. Kara, J.R. Davy, D. Goodeve, and J. Nash, editors, *Communication Skeletons*. IOS Press, Amsterdam, 1996.

[222] D.B. Skillicorn and W. Cai. A cost calculus for parallel functional programming. *Journal of Parallel and Distributed Computing*, **28**(1):65–83, July 1995.

[223] D.B. Skillicorn, Jonathon M.D. Hill, and W.F. McColl. Questions and answers about BSP. *Scientific Programming*, **6**(3):249–274, 199.

[224] J.E. Smith and W.R. Taylor. Accurate modeling of interconnection networks in vector supercomputers. In *Proceedings of the 5th ACM International Conference on Supercomputing*, pages 264–272, 1991.

[225] A. Snavely, N. Wolter, and L. Carrington. Modeling application performance by convolving machine signatures with application profiles. In *IEEE 4th Annual Workshop on Workload Characterisation*, December 2002.

[226] A. Snavely, N. Wolter, L. Carrington, R. Badia, J. Labarta, and A. Purkasthaya. A framework to enable performance modeling and prediction. In *Proceedings of Supercomputing*, 2002.

[227] Quinn Snell, Glenn Judd, and Mark Clement. Load balancing in a heterogeneous supercomputing environment. In *Proceedings of the International Conference on Parallel and Distributed Processing Techniques and Applications*, volume **2**, pages 951–957, 1998.

[228] L. Snyder. Type architectures, shared memory, and the corollary of modest potential. *Annual Review of Computer Science*, pages 289–317, 1986.

[229] F. Sötz. A method for performance prediction of parallel programs. In *Proceedings of CON-PAR 90-VAPP IV (LNCS 457)*, pages 98–107, 1990.

[230] Standard Performance Evaluation Corporation. The SPEC benchmark suite. *SPEC Newsletter*, **2**(1), 1990.

[231] M. Steed and M. Clement. Performance prediction of PVM programs. In *Proceedings of the 10th IEEE International Parallel Processing Symposium*, pages 803–807, April 1996.

[232] Thomas Sterling, Donald J. Becker, Michael R. Berry, Daniel Savarese, and Chance Reschke. Achieving a balanced low-cost architecture for mass storage management through multiple fast Ethernet channels on the Beowulf parallel workstation. In *Proceedings of the 10th IEEE International Parallel Processing Symposium*, 1996.

[233] Thomas Sterling, Donald J. Becker, and Daniel Savarese. Beowulf: A parallel workstation for scientific computation. In *Proceedings of the International Conference on Parallel Processing*, 1995.

[234] Thomas Sterling, Donald J. Becker, Daniel Savarese, Bruce Fryxell, and Kevin Olson. Communication overhead for space science applications on the Beowulf parallel workstation. In *Proceedings of the 4th International Symposium on High Performance Distributed Computing*, 1995.

[235] B. Stramm and F. Berman. Predicting the performance of large programs on scalable multicomputers. In *Proceedings of the Scalable High Performance Computing Conference*, pages 22–29, April 1992.

[236] Theodore B. Tabe, Janis Hardwick, and Quentin F. Stout. Statistical analysis of communication time on the IBM SP2. *Computing Science and Statistics*, **27**:347–351, 1995.

[237] Anthony Tam Tat Chun. *Performance Studies of High-Speed Communication on Commodity Cluster*. PhD thesis, University of Hong Kong, December 2001.

[238] Anthony Tam Tat Chun and Cho-Li Wang. Realistic communication model for parallel computing on cluster. In *Proceedings of the International Workshop on Cluster Computing*, pages 92–101, 1999.

[239] Athar B. Tayyab and Jon G. Kuhl. Stochastic performance models of parallel task systems. In *Proceedings of the ACM SIGMETRICS Conference on Measurement and Modeling of Computer Systems*, pages 284–285, 1994.

[240] P. de la Torre and C.P. Kruskal. Submachine locality in the bulk synchronous setting. In *Proceedings of the 2nd International Euro-Par Conference (LNCS 1124)*, 1996.

[241] D. Towsley, G. Rommel, and A. Stankovic. Analysis of fork-join program response times. *IEEE Transactions on Parallel and Distributed Systems*, **1**(3):286–303, July 1990.

[242] T. Tsuei and M.K. Vernon. Diagnosing parallel program speedup limitations using resource contention models. In *Proceedings of the International Conference on Parallel Processing*, volume **2**, pages 185–189, 1990.

[243] L.G. Valiant. A bridging model for parallel computation. *Communications of the ACM*, **33**(8):103–111, August 1990.

[244] A.J.C. van Gemund. *Performance Modeling of Parallel Systems*. PhD thesis, Delft University of Technology, Information Technology and Systems, April 1996.

[245] Kees van Reeuwijk, Arjan J.C. van Gemund, and Henk J. Sips. Spar: A programming language for semi-automatic compilation of parallel programs. *Concurrency: Practice and Experience*, **9**(11):1193–1205, 1997.

[246] F.A. Vaughan, D.A. Grove, and P.D. Coddington. Communication performance issues in two high performance cluster computers. In *Proceedings of the Australian Computer Science Conference*, February 2003.

[247] B. Veltman, B.J. Lageweg, and J.K. Lenstra. Multiprocessor scheduling with communication delays. *Parallel Computing*, **16**:173–182, 1990.

[248] Virtutech. Simics home page. Available from http://www.simics.com/.

[249] D.F. Vrsalovic, D.P. Siewiorek, Z.Z. Segall, and E.F. Gehringer. Performance prediction and calibration for a class of multiprocessors. *IEEE Transactions on Computers*, **37**(11):1353–1365, November 1988.

[250] H. Wabnig and G. Haring. PAPS - the parallel program performance prediction toolset. In *Proceedings of Computer Performance Evaluation: Modelling Techniques and Tools (LNCS 794)*, May 1994.

[251] Michael S. Warren, Donald J. Becker, M. Patrick Goda, John K. Salmon, and Thomas Sterling. Parallel supercomputing with commodity components. In *Proceedings of the International Conference on Parallel and Distributed Processing Techniques and Applications*, pages 1372–1381, 1997.

[252] Yuhon Wen and Geoffrey C. Fox. A performance estimator for parallel hierarchical memory systems - PetaSIM. In *Proceedings of Parallel and Distributed Systems*, pages 205–210, August 1999.

[253] R. Clint Whaley. Installing and testing the BLACSv1.1, May 1997.

[254] Frederick Wong, Richard Martin, Rmezi Arpaci-Dusseau, and David Culler. Architectural requirements and scalability of the NAS parallel benchmarks. In *Proceedings of the Conference on High Performance Networking and Computing*, November 1999.

[255] J. Worlton. Towards a taxonomy of performance metrics. *Parallel Computing*, **17**:1073–1092, 1991.

[256] Y. Yang, X. Zhang, and Y. Song. An effective and practical performance prediction model for parallel computing on non-dedicated heterogeneous NOW. *Journal of Parallel and Distributed Computing*, **38**(1):63–80, October 1996.

[257] N. Yazici-Pekergin and J.M. Vincent. Stochastic bounds on execution times of parallel programs. *IEEE Transactions on Software Engineering*, **17**:1005–1012, October 1991.

Index

A

abstraction, 2, 24, 33, 34, 39, 55
accounting, 19, 20, 65
aggregation, 50
algorithm, vii, 1, 21, 22, 27, 29, 34, 38, 39, 53, 56, 57, 62, 68, 82, 92, 95
assignment, 20, 90
assumptions, 47, 48, 56
automata, 10, 89
automation, 15

B

bandwidth, 8, 14, 19, 20, 21, 34, 48, 62, 65, 67, 71, 75, 77, 86, 105
banks, 58
benchmarking, 17, 18, 43, 57, 80, 81, 83, 99, 101, 102, 109
benchmarks, 44, 65, 67, 68, 81, 85, 90, 94, 115
binary decision, 10
blocks, 2, 17, 30, 39, 56, 62
bounds, 5, 13, 25, 30, 53, 56, 58, 59, 115
breakdown, 35
buffer, 14, 31, 71, 78
building blocks, 39
by-products, 54

C

calculus, 38, 57, 58, 105, 112
calibration, 59, 115
case study, 108
channels, 113
clusters, 81, 84, 93, 96
codes, 23, 27, 48, 63, 65, 79, 84, 85, 86
commodity, 45, 83, 91, 115
communication, 7, 9, 10, 13, 14, 15, 19, 20, 22, 23, 24, 27, 28, 29, 30, 33, 34, 35, 38, 39, 40, 43, 44, 45, 47, 48, 49, 50, 52, 53, 57, 59, 61, 62, 63, 64, 65, 68, 71, 73, 74, 75, 77, 78, 80, 81, 82, 83, 84, 86, 89, 98, 99, 100, 101, 102, 105, 107, 111, 113, 114
compilation, vii, 114
compiler, 17, 33, 34, 38, 39, 48, 78, 84
complexity, 1, 10, 11, 13, 21, 24, 28, 30, 52, 55, 57, 79
components, 24, 38, 115
composition, 9
computation, 1, 7, 13, 14, 15, 19, 20, 22, 24, 29, 30, 34, 35, 39, 41, 48, 49, 55, 56, 58, 61, 64, 65, 68, 73, 74, 80, 83, 93, 94, 101, 102, 103, 104, 107, 113, 114
computer systems, 77, 85, 92

computing, vii, 1, 2, 24, 30, 52, 87, 90, 91, 93, 94, 95, 96, 97, 104, 105, 113, 115
concurrency, 9, 94
construction, 10, 38, 54
control, 1, 2, 19, 24, 31, 34, 39, 50, 55, 56, 57, 58, 59, 64, 95
costs, 1, 8, 24, 29, 38, 71, 100
CPU, 29, 31, 61, 62, 67
cycles, 41, 42, 94

D

data distribution, 30
data set, 23, 28
data structure, 28, 47
data transfer, 13
decisions, 14, 23, 33, 38, 88, 91
decomposition, 33, 38
degradation, 2, 41, 44, 45
Department of Energy, 85
designers, 78
determinism, 35, 53, 55, 56, 61, 63, 73, 74
direct measure, 21, 59
directives, 58, 80, 83, 84
distributed applications, 98, 102
distributed computing, 92, 96, 112
distributed memory, 15, 31, 93, 99, 107
distributed memory machines, 31
distributed memory parallel computers, 99
distribution, 44, 45, 54, 56, 59, 81
duration, 14, 30, 31

E

environment, 44, 91, 103, 112
event logs, 42, 85
exclusion, 53, 55, 56, 57, 58
execution, 14, 15, 17, 18, 21, 24, 25, 33, 34, 35, 47, 49, 53, 56, 59, 62, 63, 64, 65, 69, 72, 73, 74, 75, 77, 79, 80, 84, 89, 95, 97, 110, 115
extraction, 30

extrapolation, 64

F

feedback, 73
functional programming, 112

G

generation, 86, 97, 107
graph, 24, 33, 34, 54, 55, 56, 91
grids, 27, 91
groups, 51

H

histogram, 44
HPC, 85, 92, 93, 98, 100
hybrid, 53, 56

I

implementation, 14, 38, 39, 51
inclusion, 10
independence, 37
insight, 2, 3, 14, 44, 57
instruction, 7, 30, 54, 63, 64, 65, 77
interaction, 49, 50, 73, 90, 111
interval, 47
intervention, 59, 84
iteration, 34, 48, 49, 64

J

jobs, 35

L

labour, 51
language, 30, 38, 52, 56, 79, 80, 94, 114

Index

latency, 8, 19, 20, 21, 34, 44, 48, 62, 65, 67, 75, 77, 82, 86, 89, 105
limitation, 10, 17, 23, 44, 61
linear model, 47, 48
links, 29, 34, 62
load imbalance, 22, 45, 62, 80
logging, 42

M

management, 8, 14, 31, 93, 113
manipulation, 21, 47
mapping, 29, 92, 106
Markov chain, 56
matrix, 48, 53, 64
measurement, 51, 98
measures, 38, 39, 81
memory, vii, 1, 7, 8, 13, 19, 20, 27, 28, 31, 33, 34, 54, 58, 61, 63, 64, 65, 67, 71, 73, 77, 85, 86, 101, 102, 112, 115
memory capacity, 28
message passing, 98, 110
message-passing programs, 25, 30, 31, 33, 37, 61, 73, 75, 99, 106
messages, 13, 19, 20, 30, 42, 56, 62, 67, 73, 74, 75, 81, 82
Microsoft, 94
modeling, 89, 90, 91, 93, 103, 105, 106, 107, 112
modules, 106
movement, 64, 71
MPI, 14, 37, 38, 39, 59, 61, 64, 74, 79, 81, 82, 83, 84, 85, 89, 91, 98, 99, 100, 101, 105, 107, 109, 111
multiplication, 13, 48

N

NATO, 92
network, 8, 10, 14, 19, 21, 22, 31, 34, 35, 44, 56, 61, 62, 65, 67, 71, 72, 73, 75, 77, 78, 83, 84, 86, 90, 96, 106, 109, 110
nodes, 19, 24, 34, 54, 61, 67, 68, 71, 81, 84
normal distribution, 47

O

observations, 44
operating system, 31, 44, 67, 71, 77, 78, 82
operator, 10, 56, 58, 59
order, 2, 8, 10, 15, 17, 19, 21, 22, 27, 29, 30, 50, 52, 55, 58, 59, 61, 62, 64, 74, 77, 81
orthogonality, 41
outliers, 44, 82

P

parallel algorithm, vii, 1, 20, 21, 27, 78, 90, 98, 103, 111
parallel cluster, 67
parallel performance, 69, 93, 101, 104
parallel processing, 1, 5, 7, 97, 106, 107
parallel simulation, 90, 107
parallelism, 7, 17, 24, 27, 39, 42, 52, 55, 62, 80, 92, 109
parallelization, 96
parameter, 13, 14, 20, 30, 35, 42, 48, 51, 57, 58, 59, 67, 82, 96
parameter estimation, 30
parameters, 2, 9, 14, 15, 19, 21, 24, 34, 47, 48, 51, 53, 57, 58, 59, 61, 62, 69, 75, 77, 82, 102
path analysis, 58, 62
performance benchmarking, 83
performance modelling, 2, 3, 10, 11, 15, 17, 18, 23, 41, 52, 55, 69, 74, 75, 79, 84, 85, 86, 87, 99, 101
polling, 50, 72
power, vii, 52, 56, 79, 109
prediction, viii, 8, 13, 23, 35, 41, 51, 52, 59, 69, 78, 79, 83, 85, 90, 91, 92, 93, 94, 96, 97, 98, 100, 104, 105, 106, 107, 110, 111, 112, 113, 115
probability, 31, 59, 69, 80, 81, 82, 99

probability distribution, 69, 80, 81, 82, 99
production, 111
program, 2, 3, 5, 14, 15, 17, 18, 19, 23, 24, 25, 27, 29, 30, 34, 35, 37, 38, 39, 41, 42, 44, 47, 48, 49, 51, 52, 53, 54, 55, 56, 57, 58, 59, 61, 62, 63, 64, 65, 68, 69, 73, 74, 77, 79, 80, 81, 83, 85, 95, 97, 103, 110, 114, 115
programming, 2, 7, 19, 20, 27, 33, 37, 38, 39, 42, 51, 56, 79, 95, 102, 114
protocol, 84
PVM, 37, 48, 64, 91, 93, 97, 98, 109, 113

R

range, 51, 53, 82, 83, 87
reality, 8, 23, 41, 52
reason, 9, 63, 78
relationship, 52, 92, 96
repetitions, 44, 81
replication, 52, 54
resolution, 7, 43, 81
resources, 34, 37, 52, 58
response time, 110, 114
routines, 59, 74
routing, 8, 14

S

scheduling, 31, 58, 63, 73, 114
schema, 103, 111
semantics, 7, 9, 38, 111
sensitivity, 48, 52, 62
serial code, 63, 86
shape, 47, 82, 83
sharing, 65, 104
short run, 74
signals, 43
simulation, 29, 51, 57, 58, 63, 64, 67, 69, 73, 75, 77, 80, 84, 92, 101, 104, 108
skeleton, 39

skewness, 69
software, 37, 38, 39, 51, 79, 82
space, 25, 42, 62, 67, 78, 92, 113
space-time, 62
spectrum, 17
speed, 21, 35, 67, 73, 78, 84
statistics, 35, 62
stochastic model, 23
storage, 28, 113
strategies, 33
symmetry, 52

T

task graphs, 24, 53, 56
taxonomy, 115
TCAS, 57
timing, 10, 44, 53, 61, 64, 77, 81, 111
topology, 39, 67, 75, 81
trade, 42, 51, 67, 91
trade-off, 42, 51, 67, 91
transformation, 38
transitions, 10, 56
transmission, 20, 34

V

validation, 9, 35, 82
variability, 47, 69, 81, 96
variables, 31, 34, 64
variance, 23, 24, 43, 44, 45, 47, 69, 106, 110
vector, 15, 112
visualization, 101

W

workload, 67, 107
workstation, 61, 64, 109, 113